THE

BEGINNINGS

OF

CHINESE

CIVILIZATION

THREE LECTURES
ILLUSTRATED WITH
FINDS AT ANYANG

The

Beginnings

of

Chinese

Civilization

THREE LECTURES
ILLUSTRATED WITH
FINDS AT ANYANG

By Li Chi

University of Washington Press
SEATTLE AND LONDON

THE BEGINNINGS OF CHINESE
CIVILIZATION is Number 6 of the
Far Eastern and Russian Institute
Publications on Asia. Publication was
cosponsored by the Seattle Art Museum.

Foreword

THE ORIGIN OF CHINESE CUL-
ture is paralleled in importance only by the rise of civilizations
around the eastern Mediterranean and in the Middle East. Sys-
tematic investigation of the early Mediterranean cultures was well
developed during the nineteenth century. The cultures of the
Middle East, including the Indus Valley, were rediscovered by
archaeological work only in the twentieth century. Our first con-
crete evidence of a literate early bronze age in China was discovered at the turn of this century when oracle bones found at
Anyang were recognized as authentic inscriptions in the Chinese
language written by the people of the Shang dynasty.

Oracle bones were made from the scapulae of cattle or from

tortoise shells, which were flattened and carved. On the faces of the oracle bones, diviners inscribed questions addressed to the spirits. Heat was applied to the back of the bone or shell, and an answer to the question was determined by the character of the T-shaped cracks that appeared on the face. During the nineteenth century, these bones were collected for medical purposes. They were known as "dragon bones" to old-fashioned Chinese druggists and physicians, who ground them into powder which was prescribed for nervous disorders. When it was discovered that "dragon bones" bore archaic characters of the Chinese language, an interest was aroused in China far exceeding our current curiosity concerning the discovery and translation of the Dead Sea scrolls. At first even Chinese palaeographers could make out only a word here and there. After much patient work by a large number of Chinese and a few Occidental scholars, the bone inscriptions were read, but some skeptics still doubted their authenticity. It was not until after the first scientific excavations were begun at Anyang under the direction of Dr. Li Chi that the inscriptions were proved genuine.

The archaeological site of Anyang is the largest and most important in China. Grave robbers and the curio dealers for whom they worked had for many years used it as a great mine for bronze artifacts. The prohibitions against disturbing ancestral graves in China, plus the obvious commercial advantages of such an excellent source of antiquities, worked hand in hand to keep Anyang a place of mystery. It was the interest in the inscribed bones which came from the same site that led to Dr. Li Chi's opportunity to excavate it scientifically. The significance of Dr. Li Chi's work as director of the excavations at Anyang can be compared with that of Heinrich Schliemann's excavations at the site of Troy. For, through the evidence obtained from one monumental excavation, the legendary Shang dynasty passed from the status of heroic myth to that of documented history, just as the age of Agamemnon, Menelaus, Helen, and Hector came to be recognized as fact rather than fiction as a result of Schliemann's work.

In training and background, however, Schliemann and Dr. Li Chi were entirely different. Heinrich Schliemann was a wealthy amateur inspired with the romance of archaeological investigation but lacking professional or scientific training. Dr. Li Chi began his excavating career supported by sound academic training in anthropology and archaeology. He received his Ph.D. in anthropology at Harvard in 1923. From 1925 to 1928 he was Professor of Anthropology and Archaeology at Tsinghua Research Institute, Peking. In 1928 he gave up his post at Tsinghua to become Fellow and Head of the Archaeology Section, Institute of History and Philology, Academia Sinica, a position he still holds. This new position gave Dr. Li Chi the opportunity to excavate Anyang. In 1937, after nine years of excavation, Dr. Li Chi was forced to suspend archaeological work on this site; however, he continued his studies, contributing much to our literature on Chinese culture both as an author and as editor of three important periodicals, *Archaeologia Sinica*, the *Chinese Journal of Archaeology*, and the *Bulletin of the Department of Archaeology and Anthropology, National Taiwan University*. Since 1950 Dr. Li Chi has been Head of the Department of Archaeology and Anthropology, National Taiwan University.

The bulk of Dr. Li Chi's work has been published in Chinese, and, although well known and highly respected by scholars, it has not been readily available to American or European students except as quoted in Western language publications. Therefore, his leave of absence from National Taiwan University, which made possible his lecturing in English as a Walker-Ames Professor at the University of Washington, was of the greatest importance. The three Walker-Ames lectures, sponsored by the University of Washington Far Eastern and Russian Institute in cooperation with the Seattle Art Museum in February and March of 1955,

Foreword

presented Dr. Li Chi's mature personal judgment on the important historical problem to which his life has been devoted. These public lectures constituted a singular contribution as a summary of his vast knowledge. The lectures were profusely illustrated with photographs, maps, charts, and diagrams. In this written version of the lectures, Dr. Li Chi has employed only the most significant of these illustrations. But, because many of his photographs are extremely important source materials in themselves, he has most generously included a large number of them as supplementary plates. Portions of this monograph have been published by Dr. Li Chi in Chinese; other materials appear here for the first time in any language.

MILLARD ROGERS

Seattle Art Museum
Seattle, Washington

Preface

Archaeological excava-
tion of the ancient capital of the Shang dynasty (also known as
Yin, Shang-Yin, and Yin-Shang in various writings) in the Anyang
district started in the winter of 1928 under the auspices of the
Institute of History and Philology of the Academia Sinica. The
work was carried on almost uninterruptedly until the summer of
1937, when the Japanese invasion of North China put a full stop
to this highly important but only half-finished investigation in the
field.

During the war the bulk of the collection from Anyang followed
the migration of the Institute of History and Philology to south-
western China. Much damage was done to a number of very

valuable artifacts, and there occurred many irrecoverable losses in the course of the tortuous trekkings of the Institute, such as the enormous amount of charcoal collections, the stratified soil samples, potsherds of different periods, unclassified documents and field notes, and, above all, the death of many field workers whose firsthand observations are a real loss to Chinese archaeology.

The main portion of the Anyang finds, however, is still preserved in a more or less satisfactory state and is available for detailed study. It is scarcely necessary for me to give reasons for the delay of the report on one of the most important scientific works undertaken in modern China. In spite of the most severe handicaps under which the study of this collection is still being pursued, the editor of the *Archaeologia Sinica* series has at least succeeded in printing all the ink squeezes of the oracle bone inscriptions excavated from this site from 1928 to 1937.

My own particular interest, besides the general planning of field investigations and home studies, was first concentrated on the ceramic collection, then the stone and bone artifacts, and, recently, the bronzes. My study of the prehistorical and Anyang potteries helped me more than I had thought possible in my later work on the bronzes. Some of the results of these researches have appeared from time to time in the *Chinese Journal of Archaeology* and other bulletins—all in Chinese. The shortage of funds and the lack of a good printing press in Taipei have made it almost impossible for the editors of the *Archaeologia Sinica* series to print any of these studies in a final form as originally planned.

When I was awarded a grant by the Rockefeller Foundation in 1954 to travel in the United States and Mexico for a period of three months, my friend Professor George E. Taylor, Director of the Far Eastern and Russian Institute of the University of Washington, wrote to ask me to stay with his Institute for two quarters as a Walker-Ames Visiting Professor, to meet advanced students in seminar as well as to deliver a series of public lectures on my

Anyang studies. So I took this opportunity to put together some accounts in the English language which I had not been able to make use of since my return from a lecture tour in British universities in the winter of 1936–37.

The three lectures printed here were also given on some other occasions before I reached Seattle. Lecture I was first presented in Cambridge at the Harvard-Yenching Institute, and again in Mexico City; Lecture II was given at Columbia University and also in Mexico; and Lecture III in the Peabody Museum of Archaeology and Ethnology at Harvard. I have discussed the various problems exclusively on the basis of excavated materials.

In preparing these lectures for publication, I have received generous help from many kind friends. Dr. George E. Taylor was the first to suggest the printing of these lectures, and his proposal was supported by Dr. Richard E. Fuller and Mr. Millard Rogers of the Seattle Art Museum, as well as the faculty of the Far Eastern and Russian Institute of the University of Washington. Professor Li Fang-kuei advised me on many points after he went through the manuscript. To all these friends I am greatly indebted. The photostat section of the University of Washington helped me with their excellent service by reproducing a number of negatives from the slides for plates of this book. Dr. Ruth Krader and Professor Hellmut Wilhelm provided me with books of reference which I was unable to locate in a totally new environment. Last but not least, I wish to record my gratitude to both Professor and Mrs. Li Fang-kuei, who made my stay in Seattle of almost half a year just like home.

A number of the plates are here published for the first time. This privilege has been accorded to me by special consent of the Institute of History and Philology through its Director, Dr. Tung Tso-pin. I am most grateful to the Institute for this privilege.

LI CHI

Taipei, Taiwan

Contents

Illustrations

Illustrations

PLATES (following page 59)

SUPPLEMENTARY PLATES

THE
BEGINNINGS
OF
CHINESE
CIVILIZATION

THREE LECTURES
ILLUSTRATED WITH
FINDS AT ANYANG

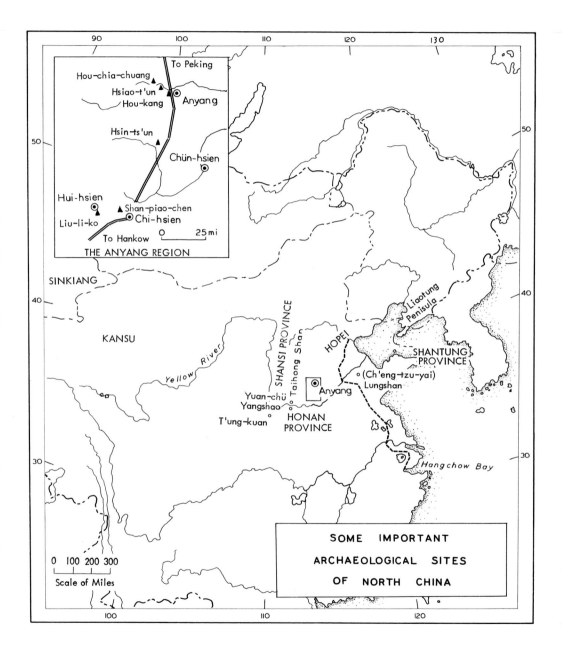

90   100   110   120   130

THE ANYANG REGION

To Peking

Hou-chia-chuang

Hsiao-t'un

Hou-kang   Anyang

Hsin-ts'un

Chün-hsien

Hui-hsien

Liu-li-ko   Shan-piao-chen   Chi-hsien

To Hankow   0   25mi

50

SINKIANG

40   KANSU

Yellow River

SHANSI PROVINCE

Taihang Shan

HOPEI   Liaotung Penisula

SHANTUNG PROVINCE

Anyang   (Ch'eng-tzu-yai)   Lungshan

Yuan-chü

Yangshao

T'ung-kuan   HONAN PROVINCE

30   Hangchow Bay

0   100   200   300
Scale of Miles

SOME   IMPORTANT

ARCHAEOLOGICAL   SITES

OF   NORTH   CHINA

100   110   120

I

Digging

Up

China's

Past

MORE THAN FORTY YEARS ago, when I was first admitted to the middle school, I used to feel extremely happy to know that I was born in a country whose history had already lasted 5,000 years. I say 5,000 years because it was actually the figure given to the youthful mind of my generation. The Sumerian civilization and the Egyptian civilization, we were told, might have started earlier; but they were also dead long ago. The Hindus, too, enjoy a long tradition, but their men of learning, till recently, never seemed to think it worth while to put their tradition on written records. So when all these things have been considered, China is certainly the oldest country still existing on this earth, and possesses the longest—and this is

3

important—continuous written history of all the nations. This was my understanding of China's past before the time of the Chinese Revolution.

After the revolution, things began to change. There was a time when the reformers of China were skeptical about everything recorded in and about the past, including history itself.[1] The Renaissance movement in the early twentieth century was essentially a rationalist movement, more or less akin in spirit to that of the classicists of the seventeenth century. Their slogan, "Show your proof," though destructive in nature, did bring about a more critical spirit in the study of ancient China. Thus, if one wants to pay excessive tribute to the Golden Age of Yao and Shun, well, Show your proof; if one wishes to talk about the engineering miracles of the Great Yü of the third millennium B.C., proofs must also be given. What must be remembered in this connection is that written records alone were no longer accepted as valid proofs.

This proof-seeking movement created a great deal of havoc with the traditional learning and revolutionized the method of classical studies. Modern archaeology in China was born in this atmosphere.[2]

The task of a modern archaeologist in China, however, is not

[1] The more important papers which reflect the spirit of this period were collected by Ku Chieh-kang in *Ku-shih-pien* (in Chinese), of which the first volume was published in 1926. Ku wrote a lengthy preface to this unique publication; it is mainly autobiographical, dealing with the development of his own interest in historical studies. A. W. Hummel, who translated this preface into English with the title *The Autobiography of a Chinese Historian*, said in the introductory remarks to his translation: "It is a critical résumé of all the currents of thought that have swept over China in the past thirty years." Hummel's translation was published in 1931 in the Sinica Leidensia Series.

[2] In the *Bulletin of the National Research Institute of History and Philology of the Academia Sinica* (in Chinese), Vol. I, No. 1 (1928), Fu Ssu-nien, the founder and the first director of the Institute, discussed in the publication notice of the bulletin the general background of historical researches in China and expounded the urgency and necessity of the adoption of a new method and a new approach for the continuous advancement of this branch of Chinese learning.

4

limited to the search for proofs in order to reinstate the glories that were China's past. His more important mission is rather to answer a set of new questions conceived in the light of modern science but only dimly perceived by historians of bygone generations. The questions so raised are of two different categories but are closely interwoven with each other: the one is concerned with the origin and the formation of the Chinese people, and the other with the nature and the building of Chinese civilization.

So the new historians have been continually asking: Who were the earliest Chinese and in what manner was the Chinese civilization developed? I shall make an attempt to answer the above two questions in a general way and on the basis of modern archaeological discoveries. Let me take up the racial history of the Chinese people first.

The earliest examples of *Homo sapiens* discovered in the Chinese area are still those from the Upper Cave of Chou-kou-tien, first found in 1933 and briefly described in a preliminary report by Franz Weidenreich in 1939.[3] The skeletal remains from this cave show a curious combination of several specimens. According to Weidenreich's descriptions, the three best preserved skulls represent "three different racial elements . . . to be classified as primitive Mongoloid, Melanesoid and Eskimoid. . . ."[4] What is amazing to many an anthropologist who studied these data is the great possibility that these three individuals might have belonged to only one family, if there was at that time a family organization. Weidenreich's paper aroused some very interesting speculations in many quarters. One of the queries stimulated by this discovery

[3]Franz Weidenreich, "On the Earliest Representatives of Modern Mankind Recovered on the Soil of East Asia," *Bulletin of the Natural History Society of Peking*, XIII (1939), 161–74. For a general account, see also *Apes, Giants and Man* (Chicago, 1946) by the same author, especially Lecture IV on the "Human Races and Principles of Their Classification and Origin," pp. 67–91.

[4]Weidenreich, "On the Earliest Representatives of Modern Mankind Recovered on the Soil of East Asia," p. 170.

5

was about the possible relation of the Upper Cave skeletons to the formation of the Chinese people in historical times. According to Weidenreich's idea, if the ancestors of the modern Chinese were already existent 20,000 years ago,[5] they were certainly not represented in the Upper Cave of Chou-kou-tien. The concluding paragraph of his interesting paper published in the *Bulletin of the Natural History Society of Peking* includes the following remarks:

> As to the origin of the Chinese—in so far as it is permissible to use this designation in determining a race—the discovery of Chou-kou-tien population failed to shed any light. Even so, one cannot conclude that the Chinese did not already exist during the Upper Palaeolithic time because there is evidence that Melanesian and Eskimoid types were in existence at that time. It is possible that the Chou-kou-tien family belonged to a migrating tribe foreign to the country and that the actual settlers who attacked and exterminated them were the real representatives of that Chinese race. . . .[6]

Professor E. A. Hooton, while agreeing with Weidenreich's major diagnosis, expressed his dissension on one point. He believed that the Old Man of the Upper Cave, whom Weidenreich classified as primitive Mongoloid, ". . . looks like a primitive European White, with more than a dash of the archaic Australoid features and can be duplicated almost exactly in the skulls of modern Ainu. . . ."[7]

Professor Hooton's remark is the more interesting because it serves to link the discovery of the Upper Cave not only with modern anthropology of the Far Eastern region but also with some curious tales transmitted from early China.

[5]Professor Hallam L. Movius, Jr., of Harvard University has written to tell me that, in his opinion, "the time when this locality (that is, the Upper Cave at Chou-kou-tien) was occupied would fall closer to 10,000 B.C. than it would to 20,000 B.C. This fact is conclusively shown by the fauna."

[6]Weidenreich, "On the Earliest Representatives of Modern Mankind Recovered on the Soil of East Asia," p. 173.

[7]E. A. Hooton, *Up from the Ape* (New York, 1946), p. 402.

6

Among the strange tales told in the *Mountain and Sea Classics*, there is one story about a Hairy People in Book 17.[8] This book is devoted to the folklore of the northeastern region of the Ancient East, covering approximately the territory of modern Manchuria, eastern Siberia, and the islands of Sakhalin and Japan. The description of the *Mao-min* of this region, that is, the Hairy People, includes some statements about both their physical appearance and their food habits. An explanatory note attached to the term *Mao-min* by a fourth-century commentator says that the faces and bodies of these people were all covered with hair.[9] It is obvious that both the author of *Shan-hai-ching* (that is, the *Mountain and Sea Classics*) and its commentator must have been more or less familiar with the appearance of the *Mao-min*, as their descriptions of these people almost exactly fit the modern Ainu, still surviving in the northern part of Japan.

Even more significant than this interesting tale about the *Mao-min* is a statement occurring in the chapter on antiphrenology of Hsün-tzǔ, the great Confucian philosopher of the third century B.C. In his scathing criticism of the practice of, and the superstitious beliefs in, phrenology, Hsün-tzǔ said: "In Hung Yao's physical appearance, no skin is visible on his bodily surface . . . ," meaning that the strange appearance of Hung Yao did in no way check his eminent career.[10]

Hung Yao, as is well known to students of ancient Chinese history, was one of the ten most prominent ministers who composed the brain trust in the court of the founders of the Chou

[8]*Shan-hai-ching* (in Chinese), Part II, Book 17, p. 80. Ssu-pu-ts'ung-k'an edition (Shanghai, 1919–1929).

[9]*Ibid.*, "Notes on 'Mao-min,' " by Kuo P'o.

[10]Homer H. Dubs, *Works of Hsüntze*, in Book V, p. 69, "Against Physiognomy"; the quoted sentence is translated as, "The physiognomy of Hung Yao was such that the skin of his face could not be seen." The footnote attached to this sentence says, "too hairy." The above work was published in 1928 in Probsthain's Oriental Series (London) as Vol. XVI.

dynasty.[11] If his face was all covered with hair, it would be by no means too speculative to take him as one of the kinsmen of the Ainu's ancestors or, perhaps, a descendant of the Old Man of the Chou-kou-tien Upper Cave, if one were inclined to accept the opinions of the late Professor Hooton. Since the Ainu have been classified as one of the Palaeo-Asiatic peoples, the assumption is certainly well justified that they played an important role in the formation of the Chinese people in the protohistorical period. But evidently they were in a small minority, as in the time of Hsün-tzǔ their hairiness was already considered more or less unusual.

As to the Melanesian elements, it is also interesting to speculate as to when they became "exterminated" by representatives of the Chinese, as Dr. Weidenreich has put it. We know almost for certain that there were still Negrito survivals in South China as late as the ninth century A.D.,[12] and perhaps even later, a fact that tends, indirectly at least, to confirm what the French archaeologists found in the prehistorical sites of Indo-China, the presence of pre-Melanesian skulls. On ancient Chinese bronzes, one occasionally finds, among their profuse decorative patterns, the casting of the human face realistically done; the Melanesian appearance is by no means rare. The most illuminating example is from the Sumitomo's collection,[13] a yu wine vase cast in the form of a tiger embracing a child; the face of the child shows a decidedly Negroid countenance with which the designer of this bronze must have been intimately acquainted. A big bronze tetrapod, weighing many hundred pounds, was dug out during World War II by a

[11]Édouard Chavannes, *Les Mémoires historiques de Se-Ma-Ts'ien* (Paris, 1895–1905), I, chap. iv, "Les Tcheou," 217–18.

[12]See, for instance, Arthur Waley's *The Life and Times of Po Chü-i* (London, 1949), p. 66; on the people of Tao-chou, the author commented, "The population was largely aboriginal and the dwarfs were perhaps Negrito similar to those of modern Malaya."

[13]This well-known specimen has been reproduced in many of the European and American catalogs on Chinese bronzes. Albert J. Koop's *Early Chinese Bronzes* (London, 1924) gives a good reproduction in Pl. XVI.

group of peasants in the neighborhood of the ancient capital of the Shang dynasty. This, too, shows, on the two standing lugs above the rim, a decorative pattern consisting of a human head, Negroid in appearance, placed between the heads of two tigers standing on their hind legs and arranged antithetically (Pl. I, 1). Other instances of this kind need not be repeated.

But down to the close of the Neolithic time in North China, the people who dominated this area were Mongoloid and, according to the study of Davidson Black, "conformed to a type essentially similar to that represented by the present-day Northern Chinese . . . ." Three years later Black again said, in the concluding chapter of his study on the Kansu and Honan Aëneolithic skulls:

> . . . As a result of the foregoing investigations into the group measurements and form relations of the Honan and Kansu prehistoric crania in comparison with recent North China material, it would seem to be established beyond any reasonable doubt that the prehistoric populations represented were essentially oriental in physical character.
>
> Further, the resemblances between these prehistoric and recent North China populations would appear to be such that the term "proto-Chinese" may with some propriety be applied to the former.[14]

It is to be observed that from the time of the Old Man of the Upper Cave of Chou-kou-tien to the Late Neolithic of North China, the time interval is more than 10,000 years. Modern archaeology has not yet been able to supply any material for a study regarding the emergence of the proto-Chinese or to fill up the gap with an evolutionary series of the Mongolian race from

[14]Davidson Black, "A Study of Kansu and Honan Aëneolithic Skulls and Specimens from Later Kansu Prehistoric Sites in Comparison with North China and Other Recent Crania," *Palaeontologia Sinica*, Ser. D, Vol. VI, Fasc. 1 (1928), p. 81. See also Black's earlier report in 1925, "On the Human Skeletal Remains from Yangshao Ts'un in Comparison with Recent North China Skeletal Materials," *Palaeontologia Sinica*, Ser. D, Vol. I, Fasc. 3 (1925), p. 98.

the primitive Mongoloid to the formation of the Chinese people in historical time, except for the find of a single tooth of Upper Palaeolithic time in the Ordos region,[15] discovered by Licent and Teilhard de Chardin, and described by Davidson Black as a "shovel-shaped upper incisor."

This isolated find, on account of its unique morphological character, has aroused a great deal of interest among both anthropologists and historians. It is doubly significant because on the one hand this morphological feature seems to be related to *Sinanthropus pekinensis*, according to Franz Weidenreich, and on the other hand to the modern Chinese. Weidenreich's study on the "Dentition of Sinanthropus Pekinensis" devoted fully two pages to discussing the problem of shovel-shaped incisors in recent mankind and made the following remarks:

> As to the occurrences of these types in recent mankind, the essential point is not that they may be found to a certain extent in all races in a minor percentage, but that they occur in special races up to almost 100 per cent; as, for instance, in Eskimo and Chinese, at least as far as the lateral incisors are concerned; and the same percentage must be taken to be characteristic for Sinanthropus . . .[16]

It is not my purpose to discuss any possible relation between the *Sinanthropus* and the Mongoloid or the Chinese. But it is important to note that Professor Weidenreich's statement about the frequency of the shovel-shaped incisors among the Chinese has recently been confirmed by an examination of the incisor teeth of freshmen of the National Taiwan University.[17] Among 803

[15]E. Licent, Teilhard de Chardin, and Davidson Black, "On a Presumably Pleistocene Human Tooth from the Sjara-osso-gol Deposits," *Bulletin of the Geological Society of China* (in Chinese), V, No. 1 (1926), 285–90.

[16] Franz Weidenreich, "Dentition of Sinanthropus Pekinensis," *Palaeontologia Sinica*, New Ser. D, No. 1 (1937), introductory chapter.

[17]Chang Kwang-chih, "Notes on Some Anthropometrical Measurements of the Freshmen of the National Taiwan University," *Bulletin of the Department of Archaeology and Anthropology* (in Chinese), No. 3 (1954), p. 43, gives a tabulated summary of percentages of occurrence of the shovel-shaped incisors.

male freshman students examined in 1952, more than 90 per cent possessed shovel-shaped upper incisors; the same was true of 121 female freshmen. In both sexes the incisors of less than 1 per cent showed a non-shovel-shaped appearance.

In addition to the above confirmatory evidence it is to be further noted that Davidson Black, in his note on the Ordos tooth, made use of a number of the upper lateral incisors recovered from the Aëneolithic sites in North China for comparative study. He said that in all these specimens, whether Early Bronze and Copper Age or modern North China, we are dealing with well-formed incisor teeth, conforming in all essentials and most details to a type aptly described by Hrdlička as shovel-shaped.

Thus modern archaeology and modern anthropology have jointly established a case that in Eastern Asia the evolution of Hominidae, from the time of early Pleistocene down to the modern age, is accompanied at different stages by a persistent morphological characterization: the invariable presence of the shovel-shaped upper incisor teeth. It is a phenomenon quite peculiar to this region, which so far has found no parallel anywhere else (Fig. 1).

There seems to be little question that the origin of the ancestors of the Chinese is tied up with the origin of the Mongoloid; and the Mongoloid race, on the evidence now available, must have evolved east of the Ural Mountains. With this background as a

a   b   c

FIG. 1. *Three examples of shovel-shaped incisor teeth from North China: a, Ordos tooth of presumably Pleistocene period; b, Sinanthropus teeth; c, upper frontal incisors of a Shang dynasty skull*

working hypothesis, we should be better prepared for an interpretation of early Chinese history.

I propose to start the discussion of early Chinese history with the Neolithic phase, as it is only at this stage that there is something definite to work upon.

It is well known that prehistorical researches in China started with the Swedish geologist, Dr. J. G. Andersson, who not only discovered the locality of Chou-kou-tien and the first trace of Peking Man but was also the first scientist to find the existence of a widely distributed prehistorical culture of the late Neolithic phase in North China. The interest shown in this discovery by archaeologists all the world over is mainly due to the possible relation this culture might have had with the West. This fascinating question, however, could hardly be settled at present on the basis of available data; so let us confine our discussion to the field of the Chinese area.[18]

In the last thirty years archaeologists have located the presence of the Painted Pottery culture along the major portion of the Yellow River Valley basin in North China, with, however, a marked exception in the province of Shantung. Its sphere of influence reached Manchuria in the east and Sinkiang in the west; its zone of concentration is located in the section of the Yellow River Valley between T'ung Kuan and Taihong Shan that divides the province of Honan from Shansi (see map).

It is precisely within this zone that the simplest type of painted pottery, in shape as well as in patterns of decoration, is located.[19]

[18]J. G. Andersson summarized his main archaeological works in China in a monograph published as No. 15 of the *Bulletin of the Museum of Far Eastern Antiquities* (Stockholm, 1943) under the title, "Researches into the Prehistory of the Chinese."

[19]In "Researches into the Prehistory of the Chinese," Andersson expressed the opinion that "the problem of pottery painting in the Far East does not begin with Yangshao, but with the hanging triangle of Ch'i Chia P'ing," (p. 282; Pl. XXXVII, 2). Since 1943, however, the chronological position of the Ch'i Chia remains, as interpreted by Andersson, has been definitely proved to

Liang Ssu-yung, followed by G. D. Wu, was of the opinion that the painted pottery discovered by him at Hou-kang in Anyang represented the earliest stage—at any rate earlier than the Yang-shao group. Wu went a step further and assigned definite dates to the Hou-kang cultures in his chronological table of Chinese prehistory.[20] It seems to be quite definite that, as far as present knowledge goes, neither in the northwest from Kansu to Sinkiang nor in the northeast from Hopei to the Liaotung Peninsula has there been discovered, up to the present time, any painted pottery culture simpler and more primitive than that found in Hou-kang, located in the northernmost part of Honan province.

What is particularly baffling in regard to the distribution of the Yangshao culture is its complete absence in the province of Shantung. In spite of the many efforts made by a number of archaeologists to find Neolithic remains in this peninsula, no trace of painted pottery has ever been discovered there. Shantung is China's Holy Land, not merely for the reason that Confucius was born there; it was also, as many historians would testify, the cultural center of China in the first millennium B.C. And, what is even more important, it was most probably the homeland where the culture of the Shang dynasty had its early growth.

It was precisely in this province that another phase of the prehistorical culture of North China was discovered by the young archaeologist Wu Gin Ding (G. D. Wu) in 1930, just after he was graduated from the Tsing Hua Research Institute. This phase is known as the Lungshan culture after the name of the village

be untenable by the discovery of Hsia Nai ("New Discoveries of a Ch'i Chia Culture," *Chinese Journal of Archaeology* [in Chinese], III [1948], 116–17). It may be noted here that, as early as 1938, G. D. Wu already mentioned the fact that the specimen of the Hou-kang painted pottery, first described by Liang Ssu-yung, consisting of a few parallel vertical lines, is the simplest of its kind that has been discovered in the whole of North China including Ch'i Chia P'ing. See also note 20.

[20] G. D. Wu, *Prehistoric Pottery in China* (London, 1938). See Pl. V; also the chronological table at the end of the book.

13

near which the first and the type site is located. The most characteristic feature of this culture, as of the Yangshao remains, is its pottery; but unlike the Yangshao pottery the Lungshan ceramics are mostly monochrome, of which the most distinguished group is pure black, lustrous, and thin. Subsequently it was found that this culture also covered a wide area in eastern and northeastern China,[21] extending northward to the Liaotung Peninsula[22] and southward to the delta region of Hangchow Bay.[23]

Following this discovery arose the chronological problem of the relative sequence of these two prehistorical cultures in North China as a whole. The basic work in the field that determined the time relation of these two cultures was carried out in the Anyang region by members of the Archaeological Section of the Academia Sinica. Here were discovered many sites in which three distinct types of cultural remains were found in successive deposition; they were: (1) the Painted Pottery culture, (2) the Black Pottery culture, and (3) the historical culture of the Shang dynasty, of which the white pottery has received the most attention from antiquarians.[24] In the stratified area of the Hou-kang site, three types of relations of the three different types of cultures were observed: the superposition is either the Shang over the Yangshao, or the Shang over the Lungshan, or, thirdly, the Lungshan over the Yangshao. These orders have been found to exist wherever intact stratified cultural remains have been located. The reverse of such

[21]Liang Ssu-yung, "The Lungshan Culture, a Prehistoric Phase of Chinese Civilization," *Proceedings of the Sixth Pacific Science Congress*, IV (1939), 59–79.

[22]Yang-Teou-Wa, *Archaeologia Orientalis*, Ser. B, Vol. III (1942). Fig. 27 on p. 48 of this report reproduces a photograph of the oracle bone discovered at this site, located west of Port Arthur in the southern tip of the Liaotung Peninsula.

[23]Shih Hsin-keng, *Preliminary Report on the Black Pottery Cultural Remains in the Second District in Hang Hsien* (in Chinese) (Hangchow, 1938).

[24]Liang Ssu-yung, "Preliminary Report on the Excavation at Hou-kang," in the *Preliminary Reports of Excavations at Anyang* (in Chinese), Part IV (1933), pp. 609–26.

orders was not reported in any of the excavated areas within this region. So the sequence thus determined may be given as: the Painted Pottery culture as the earliest, followed by the Black Pottery culture, and then the historical Shang culture.

But it must be made clear at once: this established sequence has its geographical limitation.

Now about the earliest historical Chinese culture, the culture of the Shang dynasty. For quite some time it was thought that, from the latest phase of the Neolithic culture discovered in North China to the earliest phase of the historical remains discovered in An-yang, there was a close and almost immediate succession. The cultural sequence established in Anyang and confirmed in a number of other places has been usually taken as a positive proof of the closeness in time of the Lungshan and the historical Shang cultures. But a more critical examination of their detailed contents, especially the pre-Shang and the Shang remains found in Hsiao-t'un, reveals the existence of a gap which might have been caused by interrupted development, a discontinuity which might be an indication of some time interval.[25]

What distinguished the historical remains of the Shang at Hsiao-t'un from the pre-Shang deposits found quite extensively in Anyang, including Hsiao-t'un, are the following six groups of cultural traits:

1. New development of ceramic industry
2. Employment of bronze to cast tools, weapons, and sacrificial vessels
3. The presence of a highly developed writing system
4. Chamber burials and human sacrifices
5. Use of chariots
6. Advanced stone carvings

[25]Li Chi, "Pre-Yin Cultural Deposits under the Surface of Hsiao-t'un," *Hsüeh Shu Hui K'an* (in Chinese), published by Academia Sinica, No. 1 (1944), pp. 1–14.

None of the above six cultural traits could be linked, as far as is known, in even a remote way to the Yangshao and the Lungshan cultures. They also differ among themselves in the degree of the suddenness of their emergence from a total obscurity in the Neolithic time to the foreground of the historical scene. Of these six groups the ceramic craft especially needs some discussion. The nine types of pottery which occurred most frequently in the Shang (Yin) stratum were all novel as compared with the pottery forms of the black pottery in the bottom deposit underneath the Shang stratum (Pl. II). The prevalent six types of the gritty and the black wares of the prehistorical period disappeared almost completely in the cultural stratum of the Shang period. The Shang potters discarded altogether the fine and delicate craft of producing the thin, lustrous, and beautifully turned black ware. They went on experimenting with some inventions of their own and introduced for the first time in the history of ceramic art the use of kaolin clay, with which they produced the famous white pottery. They also made the earliest attempt to cover the external surface of the stoneware with an extra coating of glaze. It is true that methods used by potters of the preceding periods were still continued in the Shang time to produce certain types of wares for daily use, but there was a distinct change in both the style and the method of production of the more refined articles.[26]

Of the other five cultural elements which made their first appearance in the Shang dynasty, the writing system and the bronze may be discussed together. The general impression has been that these two cultural activities seem to have started almost simultaneously. As I have tried to show in another connection, their simultaneity is more apparent than real; and both of them must have had an earlier development from which their Hsiao-t'un phase

[26]Li Chi, "Chemical Analyses of Different Types of Hsiao-t'un Potteries," *Memorial Volume of President Fu Ssu-nien* (in Chinese), published by the National Taiwan University (1952).

was evolved. Taking first the problem of the bronzes found in Hsiao-t'un, it is obvious to anyone who has examined this problem that an earlier background must be postulated in order to explain the stage of development which the bronze of Hsiao-t'un attained. Among the Hsiao-t'un remains themselves, evidence was by no means lacking to show that the history of bronze foundry in this locality is divisible into two substages; and the earlier substage may lead back to a still more primitive phase.

The writing system of the Hsiao-t'un stage as found on the oracle bones, like the Hsiao-t'un bronzes, represents a development on a comparatively advanced level. It is of course a well-known fact that the Hsiao-t'un scripts are 1,600 to 1,800 years later than the earliest Sumerian writing; and in this time interval the idea of keeping some written records might have migrated from the valley of the Tigris and Euphrates to the valley of the Yellow River. Still this does not explain how such a highly complicated system as the earliest known Chinese writing, composed of more than 2,000 characters and totally unlike the cuneiform scripts in either form or structure, should have appeared all of a sudden on Chinese soil. It is to be remembered that in the middle of the second millennium B.C., east of the Ural Mountains and the Indian peninsula, North China was the only literate spot in the whole region bordering on the Pacific. Even the most earnest diffusionist must prove his thesis by gathering evidence in the intervening region between Mesopotamia and the northeastern China plain before any convincing arguments can be made to support the idea of complete borrowing. Personally, I am more inclined to believe that the birth of all great civilizations, in the past as well as the present, is due to cultural contact. But before we accept this as true of any particular civilization, no effort should be spared to collect all available data in order to examine in detail the process of actual growth. In China's past, only a small area has been properly investigated up to the present time, and, even in this area, the task is hardly

17

half done. In fact, just when scientific data were being accumulated in the middle 1930's, the endeavor was brought to a sudden end by the Japanese invasion.

And now, after a lapse of almost twenty years since World War II started in the Far East, we are still dependent upon the materials collected in the brief span of nine years (1929–1937) when the Academia Sinica excavated in Anyang and its adjacent region. In many key areas, although there have been plenty of fruitful lootings, hardly any properly conducted archaeological excavations have taken place. There is scarcely any doubt that our urgent problem is still to look for new facts so that the sudden emergence of the bronze industry, as well as the writing system, may be explained on a more substantial basis.

II

Origin

and

Early

Development

In THE LAST THIRTY YEARS field archaeology in China has uncovered the remains of the Shang dynasty, datable to the middle and the latter part of the second millennium B.C. It has been found that Chinese civilization as represented by these remains, located in the northernmost part of Honan province and north of the Yellow River, was very advanced and had already attained maturity, with a complete mastery of the technique of casting bronze, the possession of an independent writing system, and an efficient and complicated military and political organization; it was also characterized by an abundance of material well-being, a remarkable manifestation of a highly sophisticated decorative art, an exacting social system, and a theocratic religion dominated by an excessive devotion to ancestor worship. It was a civilization full of vitality and vigor; although not without elements of cruelty and monstrosity, it had nevertheless adequately prepared the ground for the coming of a humanistic philosophy that found its ablest exponents in Confucius and his school in the following Chou dynasty.

Is the civilization of the Shang dynasty homogeneous, autochthonous, and entirely independent of outside influence? My answer to this question is an emphatic *no*. Let me discuss it in some detail.

It is a well-known fact that, at the close of the Neolithic age, North China was divided into at least two cultural zones, with a possible third one which still needs further clarification by more archaeological evidence. In a paper which I read before the Eighth Pacific Science Congress in 1953, I pointed out the fact that during this period:

> In the northwest and along the Sino-Mongolian border was the culture first developed by the Painted Pottery people, and most probably further elaborated by the Hsia, the first of the Chinese dynasties, which preceded the Shang. To this dynasty the earliest Chinese bronzes and bronze foundry were usually attributed both according to the historical narratives and the antiquarian's account. Most probably also, the people of this dynasty believed in and practiced totemism, in the light of some recent interpretations of certain folk literature that survived in the various compilations of the Chou philosophers.[1] The center of

[1] In the fifth year of Yin Kung of Lu (Duke Yin), Confucius noted the following event in *Ch'un Ch'iu:* "The duke reviewed a display of the fishermen at T'ang" (*Ch'un Ts'ew,* translated by James Legge in the Chinese Classics series, V, Part 1 [Hongkong, London, 1872], 19). In his translation of this entry, Legge followed the standard interpretation. The original meaning of this version has recently been discussed by Mr. Ch'en P'an, Research Fellow of the National Research Institute of History and Philology; Fu Ssu-nien, Director of the Institute at the time, wrote a lengthy supplementary note to this paper and advanced the interesting theory that the Chinese character wu 巫 , used in this connection and in many other ancient texts, really had the meaning that the term "totem" has in modern ethnology. Fu's paper has been

the second tradition is to be located near the Eastern Coast and was represented by the Black Pottery folk who survived in the historical time as the Eastern I, also known as the Squatting Barbarians in the early documents. . . .

But the forerunners of the Shang dynasty could not, by any historical or archaeological evidence, be positively identified with either of the above traditions. The founders of the Shang dynasty were probably the earliest Chinese who developed the kneeling posture into a sitting habit, known later among the Japanese as *seiza*. Whether they learned this from the Egyptian scribes or developed it independently remains to be investigated. It seems to be pretty certain that at first the ancestors of the Shang dynasty conquered the Eastern I and absorbed some of their art tradition; in return, they also taught them a new technique of warfare, on the condition, of course, that they should fight under their leadership. With this newly trained army, the Shang conquered the Hsia further west, and subsequently learned from the Hsia whatever was worth their while learning. So the dynastic splendor of the Shang is the result of the coalescence of three distinct cultural traditions: the Eastern I, the western Hsia, and the proto-Shang. . . .[2]

The foregoing statement was based mainly on the study of the decorative art of the Shang dynasty, especially the two fragments of human figures carved in stone, recovered respectively from the dwelling site of Hsiao-t'un and the cemetery site of Hou-chia-chuang (Pl. III), with additional confirmatory evidences from bone carvings and pottery decorations.

The economic conditions of the three types of community in the Aëneolithic and protohistorical periods—the Yangshao, that is, the Painted Pottery culture; the Lungshan, the Black Pottery culture; and the Hsiao-t'un, the Shang culture—are clearly reflected in the faunistic remains collected from these sites. The fauna of the Yangshao remains consist only of pigs, dogs, and

republished in the *Collected Papers of Fu Meng-chen* (in Chinese), IV (Taipei, 1952), 236–40.

[2]Li Chi, "Diverse Background of the Decorative Art of the Shang Dynasty," *Proceedings of the Eighth Pacific Science Congress*, I (Quezon City, Philippines, 1955), 181.

cattle; neither sheep nor horses were found.[3] In Ch'eng-tzu-yai,[4] the type site of the Black Pottery culture, the list of the animal bones includes those of pigs, dogs, sheep, oxen, and horses. In both Yangshao and Ch'eng-tzu-yai, deer were also found; whether they were domesticated or not is not clear. On the whole, bones of wild animals were rare in both of the prehistorical sites. This is certainly an indication of a quiet sedentary life, devoted entirely to agriculture and the keeping of a few domesticated animals; if there was any game hunting, it was limited to the hunting of a few deer.

But the faunistic assemblage from the Shang remains[5] at Hsiao-t'un is much more remarkable, not only for its greater variety of domesticated animals—for it includes oxen and buffalo, sheep and goats, dogs and horses, and two varieties of pigs; but there is also an impressive list of wild animals, ranging from monkeys to whales, and comprising bears, tigers, leopards, tapirs, elephants, rhinoceroses, many varieties of deer, foxes, badgers, and so forth. The whole list of the mammalian collection, including both the wild and the domesticated group, numbers no fewer than twenty-nine

---

[3]J. G. Andersson, "Researches into the Prehistory of the Chinese," *Bulletin of the Museum of Far Eastern Antiquities* (Stockholm), No. 15 (1943), pp. 42–43.

[4]Liang Ssu-yung, in the English summary of *Ch'eng-tzu-yai* (Nanking, 1934), p. 11, gives the following list of fauna for the lower horizon:

Canis familiaris L.	*Pseudaxis* cf. *hartulorum*
Lepus sp.	*Elaphurus menziesanus* Sowerby
Sus sp.	*Ovis changi* Teilhard and Young
Equus sp.	*Bos exiguus*
Hydropotes	

Compare for stratigraphical details the Chinese original in the same report, p. 91. See also *Ch'eng-tzu-yai: The Black Pottery Culture Site at Lung-shan-chen in Li-ch'eng-hsien, Shantung Province*, edited by Li Chi *et al.*, a translation by Kenneth Starr of *Archaeologia Sinica*, No. 1 (1934) (Yale Publications in Anthropology, 52 [New Haven, 1956]).

[5]P. Teilhard de Chardin and C. C. Young, "On the Mammalian Remains from the Archaeological Site of Anyang," *Palaeontologia Sinica*, Ser. C, Vol. VII, Fasc. 1 (1936).

species, according to the latest estimate of the eminent palaeon-
tologists Dr. C. C. Young and the late Pierre Teilhard de
Chardin.

The great abundance and variety of the faunistic remains from
Hsiao-t'un,[6] especially of the undomesticated group, may be taken
as an unmistakable index to the life of a people given to wild game
hunting. So it is obvious that the ruling house of the Shang
dynasty must have been somewhat different, culturally at least,
from the peasants of the Aëneolithic Yangshao and the Lungshan
periods. This is confirmable not only by the obsequies of the
members of the royal families but also by the oracle bone inscriptions. In *Archaeologia Sinica*, Number Two, IIB, 2908, there is on
record the following inscription:

> Divine on the day Wu-wu 戊午卜
> Ku made the inquiry 穀貞
> We are going to chase at "Ch'iu"; any capture? 我狩鼓禽
> Hunting on this day, (we) actually captured: 之日狩 允禽 隻鹿
> Tigers, one; 虎一
> Deer, forty; 虎四十
> Foxes, one hundred and sixty-four; 狐一百六十四
> Hornless deer, one hundred and fifty-nine; 麑一百五十九
> and so forth (Fig. 2) . . . .

Following the above records are some more inscriptions not yet
decipherable. The inscription quoted is a sufficiently clear example
that bears witness to the royal passion for hunting. This particular
record is attributed by Professor Tung Tso-pin to the reign of Wu-
ting of the fourteenth century B.C.[7] In another inscription of the

[6] C. C. Young and T. S. Liu, "Further Notes on the Mammalian Remains of
Yin-hsü, Anyang," *Chinese Journal of Archaeology* (in Chinese), IV (1949),
145–52.

[7] Tung Tso-pin, "On the Inscribed Plastron (No. 2908) Recording King
Wu-ting's Hunting Expedition to 'Ch'iu' (鼓)," *Continental Magazine*
(in Chinese), Vol. VIII, No. 12 (June, 1954).

same period, it is recorded that two tigers were captured; the largest number of deer shot in one chase during this reign is 162.[8]

Hunting records are frequently found in the oracle bone inscriptions; they were taken down from various periods and by different kings; so this passion for big game hunting was really a tribal habit shared in common by all the members of the royal house instead of being the idiosyncrasy of an individual king.

FIG. 2. *Ink rubbing of the inscribed plastron about King Wu-ting's captures in a hunting expedition at "Ch'iu"*

[8]*Ibid.*, p. 14.

24

The royal passion for sports may be also testified to by the fact that, underneath the wooden chamber where the royal coffin was placed, there were always sacrificial pits in which large dogs accompanied by big adult human males were sacrificed. These men and dogs were the king's company in his lifetime; as they followed him in his moments of pleasure, so they accompanied him to another world (Pl. IV).

Thus it could not be considered as a mere coincidence that with the coming of Shang there was a sudden efflorescence of animal art. This art must have been developed with a whole tribal tradition behind it: the passion for hunting and also for keeping wild animals alive; then, at the death of the master, all followed him to eternity. Once correlated with this tradition, the animal art of this period becomes much more intelligible.

If the Shang culture was totally different from the Yangshao and not exactly the same as the Lungshan, the question naturally arises, where was this culture first developed? The question sounds complicated, so the answer requires a ramified search.

In my paper on the "Diverse Background of the Decorative Art of the Shang Dynasty" which I have cited above, I tried to show that the animal art found on the Shang bronzes was most probably derived from wood carvings. The imprints left on the pounded earth in the royal tombs were originally the decorative parts of perishable materials, made up mostly of leather, textiles, and wood (Pl. V). Although the wooden chamber which housed the royal coffin has vanished with only minute fragments left here and there, still these are sufficient to prove that the inside of the chamber was originally decorated. So the existence of a wood-carving art is beyond dispute.[9] A study of the imprints on the pounded earth from the various tombs proves that the Chinese decorative

[9]The late Mr. Liang Ssu-yung, in his copious field notes on the Hou-chia-chuang excavations, mentioned positive evidences proving that inside the wooden chambers that housed the coffins in all the big tombs within this cemetery area there were elaborately carved and painted decorations.

art at this stage of its development was already a commingling of several traditions; a similar condition is also reflected in the bone and stone carvings. Among the sundry traditions, the one with an obvious Western affiliation usually attracts the attention of the archaeologists first. Several important examples under this category may be mentioned; of these the *fei-i* monster (Fig. 3), developed as a decorative pattern with one head, *t'ao-t'ie* fashion,

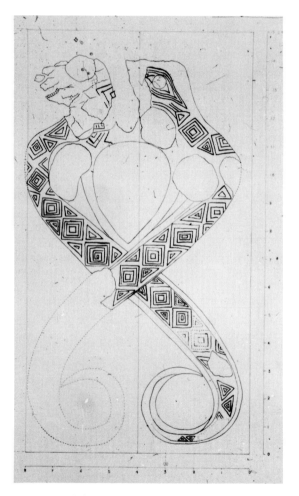

FIG. 3. Fei-i *pattern traced from the remnants of a disintegrated wooden article in one of the big tombs of Hou-chia-chuang*

and two intertwining bodies, may be taken as the first instance. This pattern was traced out on the top of the wooden chamber in HPKM: 1001 of the Hou-chia-chuang royal cemetery, and is certainly the earliest example of its kind in the art history of China. The pattern underwent an evolution in China and was transmitted in various versions in later times. It reappeared in the famous Wu Liang Tz'u's two incised human figures,[10] the lower parts of which are made up of two long tails intertwined with each other. But the earliest example of this pattern as found in the royal tomb was already more than a thousand years later than those discovered in the Middle and the Near East. So its ultimate origin must be traced to the Mesopotamian region; and it is quite likely that, like the gold-foiled handle from Gebel el Tarif of Egypt, decorated by two intertwining snakes, which Henri Frankfort thought was of Sumerian derivation,[11] the *fei-i* pattern of the Shang art was inspired from the same origin, modified to some extent to suit the Chinese tradition.

Another motif that appeared among the traces of the perishable wood-carving art is a pair of tigers, arranged antithetically with tails pointing toward the center and an animal face between the tigers near the top. The whole pattern was badly decayed and almost beyond recognition, but careful tracing work recovered it. The accuracy of the tracing was proved by the discovery of a similar pattern on a big bronze tetrapod recovered in a village very near to the royal cemetery (Pl. I, 1). This is evidently a degenerated version of the famous Hero and Beast motif, which also originated in Mesopotamia and was then transmitted to Egypt

[10]Jung Keng, *Photographic Reproductions of the Rubbings of the Tomb Figures of Wu Liang Tz'u* (in Chinese), published by the Yenching Archaeological Society, Monograph 3 (1934). See also Édouard Chavannes, *La Sculpture sur pierre en Chine au temps des deux dynasties Han* (Paris, 1893), Pl. XXIV.

[11]Henri Frankfort, *The Birth of Civilization in the Near East* (London, 1951), p. 102; Pls. X, 16, and XXI, 41.

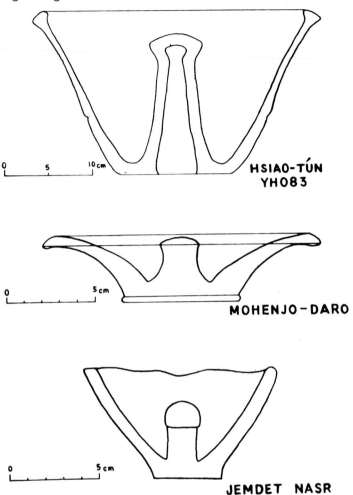

FIG. 4. *A type of jar cover found in Jemdet Nasr, Mohenjo-daro, and Hsiao-t'un.* (*The bottom one from* New Light on the Most Ancient East, *by V. Gordon Childe [New York: Frederick A. Praeger Inc., 1952], p. 132. Reproduced with permission of the publisher*)

and later immortalized in the Mycenaean time by the famous Lion Gate.[12]

It is clear that, as it appeared on the Chinese bronzes, the motif of the hero subduing the beasts had already undergone important

[12]*Ibid.*, Pl. XIII, 23, 24; p. 102.

28

changes. In place of the figure of the hero, the character *wang* (王), meaning the king, might appear; and the lions on both sides were replaced at first by tigers, and later by a pair of boars or even dogs. In some cases the hero was given an actual human figure but was also accompanied by an additional beast placed under the figure of the hero. In other cases some other character, not yet decipherable, was substituted for the pictorial character for the king. All these versions, which appeared as incised symbols on many bronzes, were, it seems to me, simply variations of the original Mesopotamian motif (Pl. I, 2–12).

The most interesting proof of China's contact with the West in the second millennium B.C. or even earlier comes from some pottery forms. The example I have in mind for illustration is a jar cover, in the shape of a flower pot, with a phallic-shaped handle standing upright in the center inside the pot. This type of cover, as made known by McKay and publicized by Gordon Childe,[13] was also found in Jemdet Nasr and Mohenjo-daro. Comparing the pottery forms of the Shang period with those of the Middle East and the Near East regions, one may find a number of instances that exhibit close resemblances; but I take this one as the most indisputable example indicating cultural contact, as no imaginable reason could be conceived for the independent invention of covers so similar in structure in two different and widely separated parts of the world (Fig. 4).

All these evidences, however, show only the existence of some contact between the cultures of the Near East and the Far East. The nature of such contact could scarcely be inferred from the above evidences; it may have been a very remote one resulting in partial imitations, such as most of the instances cited actually were. The real foundation of the Shang culture was still in the Asiatic East, which also gave rise to and inspired the major art

[13]V. Gordon Childe, *New Light on the Most Ancient East* (New York, 1952), pp. 132 ff. and Fig. 65.

tradition of the whole Pacific basin. The source of this tradition is most probably to be found in the lost art of wood carving of China's past. I have dwelt elsewhere on the main features of this particular tradition in some detail; as they are so important in the present connection, let me cite some of the samples used for the illustration of this thesis.

The unique bone handle which I first uncovered in 1929 still

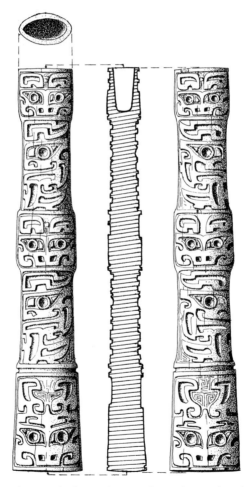

FIG. 5. *Patterns of carved decoration and sections of a bone handle from Hsiao-t'un*

remains the most important example of its kind that is nearly complete. The most remarkable features of this handle are the ornamental patterns (Fig. 5). It is about 15 cm. in length and almond-shaped crosswise, with a socket at the smaller end that measures 16 mm. deep; the cross section of the socket, which is lentil-shaped, measures 16 mm. by 8 mm. at the maximum. The outside of this handle is completely carved from top to bottom, on both sides and in five units; three of the units are composed of *t'ao-t'ie* masks, each consisting of a pair of such masks joined at the back and facing opposite sides. These three units are separated from each other by two longer and slenderer units of *t'ao-t'ie* in profile, each with a body attached to the head. These five units of decorative patterns, essentially similar to one another, pile up on the handle with a vertical succession that reminds one of the arrangements of the animal heads carved on the totem poles found on the northwestern coast of Canada, except that the composition of the Hsiao-t'un handle seems to carry a more subtle rhythm.

The decorative patterns and their arrangement described above suggest three principles which have been found to be basic in most Pacific arts; besides the piling up of similar designs in vertical succession, there are the junction of profiles of the animal body, split into two symmetrical halves on a curved surface or a flat one, and, in addition, a rigid symmetry and a regular rhythm. All these three principles found their fullest expression in the bronze works of Shang and later times and in many of the wood carvings of the Pacific region.[14]

Let me give some more examples from the excavated bronzes of Anyang. Of this collection there are many square *yi* (方彝) on record. Each of the square sides was cast like a flat piece of wooden plank (Pl. VI, left). All the sides are fully decorated with the head of an animal either with or without a body as the central motif, surrounded by some minor decorative patterns. The main theme

[14]Franz Boas, *Primitive Art* (Oslo, 1927), pp. 223 ff.

on the *yi* illustrated is the treatment of the animal's head; it is an attempt to render a three-dimensional object on a two-dimensional background by cutting the head into two profiles and joining them together in a perfectly symmetrical arrangement. The effect is almost exactly the same as that of the house-front painting of the Kwakiutl, cited by Franz Boas in his work on *Primitive Art*.[15] On the Chinese bronzes, such animal heads have been called *t'ao-t'ie*, but they evidently had more realistic names in earlier times, names more suggestive of the true nature of these animal representations.

The square *yi* of the Shang time is almost always fully decorated. In one of my earlier papers[16] I have tried to show that, as far as the shapes of the excavated bronzes from Hsiao-t'un are concerned, the majority of these in the round-bodied group derived their origin from the pottery forms, while the angular type—both the square and the quadrangular bronzes—copied their forms as well as their patterns of decoration from some wooden prototypes. It was also pointed out in this paper that the angular type was always fully decorated (Pl. VI), while the round type was fully covered only rarely, and more frequently left completely plain (Pl. VII). An obvious inference from all these discoveries would be that the angular-bodied bronzes not only inherited the shapes of the wooden prototypes but also carried on the method and patterns of decoration of the wood carvers, while the round-bodied articles cast in bronze, shaped mainly after the ceramic tradition, acquired their ornaments much later.

It may be further inferred that, as the members of the ruling house of Shang were probably all genuine lovers of wild game hunting, such habits were very likely nurtured in a forest environment, which would also be best fitted for the development of a wood-carving art. It is most interesting to compare the types of

[15] *Ibid.*, p. 239.
[16] Li Chi, "Studies of Hsiao-t'un Bronzes, Part I," *Chinese Journal of Archaeology* (in Chinese), III (1948), 69.

animal patterns on the bronzes with the hunting records in the
oracle bone inscriptions. Tiger and deer motifs were constantly
met with on the chariot pieces as well as on the big bronzes; the
tiger was frequently found on musical stones, inlaid and painted
decorative pieces, of which the substances had disappeared long
ago but whose impression had been left on the stamped earth.

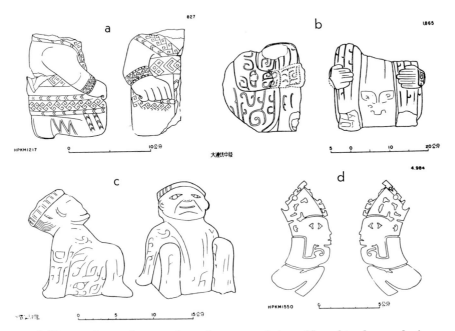

FIG. 6. *Human figures in stone from Anyang: a, d, from Hou-chia-chuang; b, from
Hsiao-t'un; c, from Ssu-p'an-mo*

The abundance of deer is proved not only by the hunting records;
it is even better testified to by their skeletal remains, quantitatively
second only to the domesticated pigs among the remains of Hsiao-
t'un. These animals, as we know, are essentially woodland crea-
tures; wherever they roamed, their presence may be taken as an
indication of some forested region not far off.

The dominance of the animal motifs, however, did not succeed
in obliterating completely the geometrical arts which prevailed

33

in North China before the Shang. Authentic Shang bronzes were sometimes covered exclusively with spirals or zigzags (Pls. VIII, below; IX, above). The most important example that testifies to the survival of geometrical decoration in the Shang dynasty is a fragment of a stone human figure in a kneeling-sitting posture, fully dressed in robe and skirt; the border of the garment and the skirt and the cuff of the sleeve are all ornamented with a band composed of double chevrons and interlocked T-patterns (Pl. III, left; Fig. 6A). All these patterns are incised in narrow lines, hardly wider than 1 mm.; most of the lines thus rendered are short and straight, and at each turning the incision usually starts anew. There is no continuous curvilinear line in the whole composition.

This kneeling-sitting posture, as distinguished from the squatting-sitting stone torso (Fig. 6B) discovered at Hsiao-t'un, is singularly significant in that it serves to link the daily habit of the ruling class of the Shang dynasty with the decorative art found at the closing phase of the Neolithic time, especially in the Black Pottery region. In the historical period, as we have noted, the indigenous inhabitants who inherited the old territory of the Black Pottery people on the eastern coast were known as the Eastern I, or the Squatting Barbarians. In other words, while the Shang people adopted the decorative art of the coastal culture to a limited extent, the native inhabitants of the coast had stuck to their old habit of squatting instead of aping the *seiza* posture of their conquerors.

The squatting torso from Hsiao-t'un, however, cannot be identified with the coastal culture, if we take the Black Pottery tradition as its main representative. Unlike the Hou-chia-chuang figure, it is entirely devoid of any sartorial covering, except perhaps an apron in the front below the waistline. All four limbs are covered by carved tattooing marks of disintegrated patterns reassembled around an eye design near the joints.

Tattooing as a cultural trait survived among many indigenous tribes south of the Yangtze River in early China. The first century B.C. historian, Ssu-ma Ch'ien, made it known that the native people of Chekiang, whose culture the uncles of the founder of the Chou dynasty adopted, practiced tattooing.[17] In the classic *Li Chi* there occurs this general statement: "The Easterners are called I (夷); they let their hair loose, and tattoo their bodies."[18] On the basis of this statement, it seems to be justifiable to identify the Hsiao-t'un torso with the squatting Eastern I; however, additional evidence is needed to show that the tattooing patterns found on the torso of Hsiao-t'un were evolved from a prehistorical prototype before such identification can be confirmed. The southern origin of this particular custom is probably indisputable, as many of the aboriginal tribes south of the Yangtze River are still tattooing their bodies.

This leads us to another aspect of the culture of the Shang dynasty as a whole. How large a portion of its total content may be considered as related to the south or of southern origin? Twenty years ago, I stated in the *Preliminary Reports of Excavations at Anyang* that the shouldered celts, tin ingots, rice, elephants, and buffalo were all apparently related to the south.[19] As the matter stands now, and after twenty years of discussion and reflection, it seems proper that the case should be restated. Rice was cultivated in northern Honan as early as the Yangshao time; however, no domesticated buffalo were discovered contemporaneous with this cultivation.[20] In the Shang time, on the other hand, according to recent interpretation of some passages in the oracle bone in-

[17]Édouard Chavannes, *Les Mémoires historiques de Se-Ma-Ts'ien* (Paris, 1895–1905), IV, chap. xxxi, "Tai-po de Ou," 2.

[18]*Li Chi,* chap. "Wang Chih," Thirteen Classics edition, XII, 12 (translated by James Legge, *The Sacred Books of China,* Part III, p. 229, in the Sacred Books of the East series, edited by F. Max Müller, Vol. XXVII [Oxford, 1885]).

[19]Li Chi, *Preliminary Reports of Excavations at Anyang* (in Chinese), Part IV (1933), p. 576.

[20]Andersson, "Researches into the Prehistory of the Chinese," pp. 43–44.

35

scriptions, not only was there rice cultivation but the fields were actually ploughed, and the ploughs were drawn by domesticated buffalo.[21] The character for rice was identified in the oracle bone inscriptions. In this connection it might be fitting to quote the authentic opinion of the authors of "On the Mammalian Remains from the Archaeological Site of Anyang." In a note at the end of their report, they said: "The discoveries from western Honan, northern Shantung, and eastern Szechwan support the idea that in Anyang, *Bubalus mephistopheles* represents an old indigenous type (artificially prolonged by domestication) rather than an imported foreign form."[22] So it would seem that, although the rice cultivation may have originated in the south, it may have been improved and further developed in the Yellow River basin. The statistical study of the faunistic remains of Hsiao-t'un by C. C. Young shows that *Bubalus mephistopheles* is one of the three mammals that ranked highest numerically in our collection, the individual specimens exceeding 1,000 in number.[23] Yet buffalo were never used for sacrificial purposes; in the sacrificial pits, only *Bos exiguus* was found.

The problem of the tin remains the same as twenty years ago; no new data can be added (Pl. X). It may be emphasized once more that the very fact that this mineral was stored in ingot form is an indication of its being imported from some distance. The copper was evidently smelted right at the spot of the foundry near the site of Hsiao-t'un, as malachite ore was more than once discovered. This ore was apparently brought to the foundry without any preliminary reduction. If the tin was imported, the further

[21]Hu Hou-hsüan, "Agricultural Records of the Yin Dynasty from the Oracle Bone Inscriptions" (in Chinese), *Chia Ku Hsüeh Shang Shih Lun Ts'ung*, II (1945), 81.

[22]See note 5, Lecture II.

[23]See note 5, Lecture II; see also Shih Chang-ju, "On the Animal Remains from the Tombs of the Yin Dynasty at Hsiao-t'un, Anyang," *Bulletin of the College of Arts* (in Chinese), published by the National Taiwan University, No. 5 (1954).

question is whether it was imported from the south or from some other quarter. Old gazetteers reported the production of tin in North China within the radius of a few hundred kilometers of Anyang.[24] Mining geologists are not totally prepared to accept such reports, but neither are they prepared to deny their accuracy altogether.

Elephants, like buffalo, might have been native Anyang beasts, too, at least in the Shang time. As for shouldered celts, they might have inspired certain types of bronze weapons of the Shang dynasty.

In addition to the 1933 list, one item of real significance should be added, namely the tortoises whose plastrons were used for divinatory purposes. My colleague Professor Shih Chang-ju recently argued for an independent origin of plastromancy,[25] as a contrast to the practice of scapulimancy of the Lungshan culture. Whether one agrees with him or not, the southern origin of *Testudo anyangensis* seems to be indisputable. If these shells were sent to the royal court as tributes from various vassal states, as abundantly proved in the oracle bone inscriptions and recently elucidated by Tung Tso-pin,[26] it is a sure proof that the Shang Empire had a large slice of territory south of the Yangtze River, over which it might have exercised some political control.

To sum up: my thesis is that the culture of the Shang dynasty is a very composite affair and represents a fusion of many cultural streams. The fundamental stratum upon which the Shang culture was built is rooted deep in the prehistorical past; the development of the rice culture and the whole complex attached to it illustrates the fact that the economic basis of the Shang Empire is typically

[24]Motonosuke Amano, "Mining and Agriculture in the Yin Dynasty," *Tôhô Gakuhô (Journal of Oriental Studies)* (Kyoto), No. 23 (1953), p. 236.

[25]Oral communications.

[26]See also M. N. Pien, "On the Turtle Remains from the Archaeological Site of Anyang, Honan," *Bulletin of the Geological Society of China*, XVII, No. 1 (1937), 121–33.

Eastern Asiatic and developed *in situ*, as shown by the various eminent workers in the field, such as Andersson, Teilhard de Chardin, and Young, and reaffirmed by the oracle bone inscriptions. The ruling house of the Shang dynasty had a passion for big game; in the royal park at Hsiao-t'un, the collection certainly included tigers, elephants, monkeys, many species of deer, foxes, wolves, wild boars, and such rare animals as *Budorcas taxicolor lichii*. Their hunting territory must have covered a very large region including large tracts of heavily forested region and extending to places like eastern Mongolia and southern Manchuria. From these quarters, and also from the eastern seaboard, the ancestors of the Shang dynasty acquired some vague knowledge of foreign countries. The Shang people might have been the earliest Chinese to make extensive use of chariots both for hunting and for war purposes, although it as as yet impossible to prove that the Shang people were the first to introduce metals. But it is beyond any doubt that they improved the art and craft of the bronze-casting industry enormously; and the chief use they made of the alloy was to cast ceremonial vessels which were never equaled in any other parts of the world.

The basic problem concerning the genesis of the Shang culture has to do with the still undiscovered pre-Shang phases of the evolution of the Chinese scripts. In this connection, it must be remembered that, so far, only a very small area of North China has been properly investigated; if other key areas could be studied as thoroughly as the valley of the Huan River, it would certainly be only a matter of time until such fundamental problems would be solved.

III

The

Bronze

Age

of China

The bronze age of china, as far as present knowledge goes, ranges from the middle of the second millennium B.C. to the middle of the first millennium B.C. Actually, of course, it lasted much more than one thousand years. But it is difficult to fix a definite date either for its beginning or for its end. In the past, students of Chinese bronzes were so completely charmed and dazzled by the splendor of the ritual vessels that they scarcely found any chance to ponder upon the possibility of a humbler history for these antiquities. But, like every other craft and institution, the bronze industry of China never was a gift from heaven; it emerged gradually and developed step by step. At least, modern archaeology is proving this to be the case.

39

STRATIGRAPHY

The most reliable set of data available for a scientific study of this problem is no doubt the collection of bronzes from the Anyang excavations. Of the various localities which were excavated in Anyang, two are the most important. They are the dwelling site of Hsiao-t'un and the cemetery site of Hou-chia-chuang. While it was from the dwelling site that practically all the written records on oracle bones were recovered,[1] it was from the tombs that the significant collections of bronzes were made. During the Shang dynasty, the northwestern part of Hou-chia-chuang was used exclusively as a burial ground. In Hsiao-t'un, burials of a sacrificial type were also discovered; although not comparable in magnitude with the Hou-chia-chuang big tombs, they were evidently contemporaneous with them. From these burials, a number of important bronzes were also recovered. So the great majority of the bronzes from Hsiao-t'un and Hou-chia-chuang are tomb furniture, buried together with one or a number of persons. Only occasionally was a hoard of bronzes discovered in a storage pit. Such hoards constitute only a small fraction of the total collection; specimens from the storage pits are not only limited in number but are also limited in typology.

For a long while, the exact relation of the tomb bronzes to the inscribed oracle bones, uncovered mainly from the cultural stratum of the Shang dynasty, at Hsiao-t'un, remained an enigma to the fieldworkers in Anyang. In fact, although more than a thousand tombs in Hou-chia-chuang and Hsiao-t'un were opened by the Anyang excavation party, none of them contained any inscribed

[1]With the exception of a small lot of inscribed oracle bones discovered in the southern part of Hou-chia-chuang (see Tung Tso-pin, "On the Seven Complete Inscribed Tortoise Shells from the Excavation at Hou-chia-chuang, Anyang," *T'ien-yeh-k'ao-ku-pao-kao* [in Chinese], No. 1 [1936], pp. 91–165), and one piece found at the site of Hou-kang, all the inscribed oracle bones in the Academia Sinica collection were excavated from the dwelling site of Hsiao-t'un.

oracle bones; a few inscribed bronzes discovered in the tombs, which seemed helpful for identification purposes, are again too meager for detailed investigation, as none of these inscriptions contains more than ten characters.[2] Thus the inscribed oracle bones and the beautiful big bronze vessels, in the opinion of the field archaeologists at Anyang, were only indirectly and partially associated.

This partial association was determined by a careful study of the content of one storage pit, E16, discovered at Hsiao-t'un in the fourth season of the Anyang expedition (1931).[3] In this pit a large number of inscribed scapulae as well as plastrons, in addition to a small hoard of well-preserved bronze tools and weapons, were found together. As weapons and tools similar in type to this hoard were also found among the burial goods of Hsiao-t'un and Hou-chia-chuang, E16 has served as a strong connecting link which definitely proves the contemporaneity of the bronze with the oracle bone records.

This link, however, connects these two cultural traits in only a general way; it supplies no details as to how closely the different stages of bronze development are related to the various periods of oracle bone inscriptions. It is fairly obvious that the industry of bronze foundry underwent a process of evolution during the time that the Shang dynasty had its capital at Hsiao-t'un. But by what criteria besides typology are these substages to be divided?

[2]Of the excavated bronzes from Hsiao-t'un and Hou-chia-chuang, only one piece bears an inscription of four characters; it is a big basin-shaped container, placed at one of the passages in one of the big tombs. The four characters read: *ch'in* (sleeping), *hsiao* (small), *shih* (chamber), and *yü* (basin). See Pl. IX, below.

[3]Storage Pit 16 was discovered and excavated in the fourth season at Hsiao-t'un in the spring of 1931; this pit was first found on April 10 of that year, and the excavation lasted nine days; the deposit reached a depth of 9.3 meters, somewhat beyond the present water level in the rainy season. The pit is circular in shape with a diameter of 1.7 meters at the upper rim. See for details *Preliminary Reports of Excavations at Anyang* (in Chinese), Part IV (1933), pp. 564–67.

The answer to this question depends much, of course, upon our knowledge of the underground condition of the occupation site at Hsiao-t'un. The earliest settlers in this place were the prehistoric Black Pottery people, who lived in huts partly underground; besides pottery, they manufactured bone and stone implements, but they possessed no knowledge of bronze or copper. This cultural stratum at Hsiao-t'un was first worked out by the Anyang excavation party; they discovered further that on and directly above this cultural stratum were the deposits of the metal-using Shang people.[4] This observation, however, is susceptible to two interpretations. It may be asked: Are the immediate successors of the Black Pottery culture at Hsiao-t'un the dynastic Shang people or their forerunners?

The establishment of Yin (namely, the locality at Hsiao-t'un) as the capital of the Shang Empire in the time of P'an Keng is an important historical event long familiar to students of antiquity and Chinese history; traditional chronology attributed its occurrence to the fifteenth year of P'an Keng's reign, which was approximately 1384 B.C.[5] Modern archaeology is naturally concerned

[4]Li Chi, "Pre-Yin Cultural Deposits under the Surface of Hsiao-t'un," *Hsüeh Shu Hui K'an* (in Chinese), published by Academia Sinica, No. 1 (1944), pp. 1–14.

[5]Recent discussions on the chronology of the Shang (Yin) dynasty have advanced much of our knowledge about its complicated nature, but the result, if there is any, is still far from being conclusive. I have in the tentative table of this paper chosen a more conservative estimate, as it seems to me that none of the half-dozen new dates proposed by the various schools is backed up by arguments either more substantial or less defective than earlier calculations. One of the most serious attempts to build up a new chronology for this period is, no doubt, the one made by Professor Homer H. Dubs. In defense of his own interpretations of astronomical records preserved in ancient Chinese documents, he has recently criticized, rather fairly I should say, Tung Tso-pin's (Dung Dzo-pin, according to Dubs) chronology in these words: "It is dangerous to employ a Han Calendar for a period a thousand years earlier" ("The Date of the Shang Period," *T'oung Pao*, XL, Nos. 4–5 [1951], 325). It is, therefore, most amazing to read in the same paper five pages further on, where the author discusses the problem of the beginning and end of "day," the following remarks: "Later Chinese practice, however, provides *strong evidence* [italics

with the problem of whether Hsiao-t'un was a deserted village or a populous city when P'an Keng cast his eye on that place and made the momentous decision to establish there the royal seat of administration. Hsiao-t'un continued as the capital city until the end of the Shang dynasty—a period of 273 years, about seven years longer than the total reign of the Manchus.

It has been assumed, on a very substantial basis, that P'an Keng's new era coincided with a series of novel architectural activities (Pl. XI), which left abundant traces among the ruins of Yin-hsü. The new method of building introduced in this new era was the adoption of pisé, which the field archaeologists in Anyang call *hang-t'u*. It is a method that is still extensively employed in all parts of China, wherever the clay is of a kind that can be stamped.

The underground deposit of Hsiao-t'un, when uncovered, exhibited extensive foundations built of pisé; around these foundations were located many sacrificial pits, in which were buried both human and animal victims, accompanied in a number of cases by bronzes, pottery, and articles of bone and jade. Underneath the pisé foundations were found many subterranean pits and caches and sometimes even the remains of dwelling floors, which were undoubtedly earlier than the overlying stratum built of *hang-t'u*. The artifacts excavated from the various pits in the substrata often

mine] that in the Shang period China used the Roman Day. Eclipse Record IV confirms that probability" (p. 330). The point is, as admitted by Professor Dubs himself, that Eclipse Record IV is also a defective document which contains at least one character, a key word for the interpretation of the whole record, still disputable as to its exact connotation. It is obvious that here Professor Dubs's superior knowledge of astronomy does not help him to settle this problem. When he goes back to the idea of referring to "later practice" as "strong evidence" to prove what might have been the case a thousand years or so earlier, or even a few hundred years earlier for that matter, he seems to be using exactly the same method which he had discredited in the earlier part of his paper. So, pending the arrival of a genuine scientific reconstruction of the Shang chronology, a more conservative date is certainly preferable for the simple reason that it would, at least, avoid much useless confusion.

show no appreciable difference from authentic Shang finds but are decidedly different when compared with the premetallic remains of the Black Pottery period.

Thus, in many respects, the transition from the predynastic Shang period to the dynastic Shang period at Hsiao-t'un happened without any concurrent changes of the material culture. The question is further complicated by the fact that the *hang-t'u* remains were built in several different periods, so it frequently happened that early dynastic Shang pits might be overlaid by late dynastic Shang *hang-t'u* buildings. It is not my purpose here to disentangle these intricate relations between the pre-Shang and dynastic Shang underground conditions. Suffice it to say that differences actually existed and have been found. Professor Shih Chang-ju, field director of the last three seasons of Academia Sinica's archaeological expedition to Anyang, says:

> The normal stratification under the surface soil of Hsiao-t'un
> is composed of subterranean pits, caches, or houses as the lower
> layer, overlaid by a stratum of *hang-t'u* foundations. There are
> many instances of this type; they are quite extensively distributed
> under the surface soil of the Hsiao-t'un site.[6]

As to the time interval that separates the two strata, Shih is of the opinion that it is, as yet, not ascertainable. Shih is also of the opinion that, before this place was chosen as the capital city, it must have been already occupied by the pioneers of the Shang settlers for a considerable length of time. The culture of the dynastic period is profusely represented by abundant archaeological remains; in addition to many magnificent bronzes, whose date we shall discuss at length, there are the oracle bones, the chariots, wooden chamber burials, and many pieces of stone, jade, bone, and ivory carvings, and so forth. Most of these can be dated on a fairly accurate basis and assigned to the period from the reign of P'an Keng to the downfall of the Shang dynasty.

[6]Translated from the unpublished manuscripts of Shih Chang-ju.

But the cultural remains do not seem to terminate at the
same time as the fall of the Shang. What followed the Chou conquest of this ancient capital has also for a long time been a matter
of speculation. According to available historical accounts, the
capital must have been thoroughly sacked by the Chou soldiers
after the last king of the Shang dynasty, King Chou, burned his
palace and his own body.[7] Ssu-ma Ch'ien put it on record that
when Chi Tzŭ, the elder brother of King Chou, who surrendered

TABLE 1

CULTURAL STAGES OF HSIAO-T'UN REMAINS

Periods	Cultural Characteristics	Stratifications	Dating
1. Premetallic	Black Pottery	Bottom layer (on the virgin soil)	Late Neolithic
2. Predynastic Shang	Early Bronze	Above Black Pottery, below *hang-t'u*	Up to about 1384 B.C.
3. Dynastic Shang	Middle Bronze I	*Hang-t'u* period	ca. 1384–1111 B.C.
4. Post-Shang	Middle Bronze II	Post-*hang-t'u*	1111 B.C.

and received a title from the new dynasty, revisited the old capital
some years after the conquest, he found only beautiful crops of
wheat or millet growing all over the ruins of the destroyed palaces
and ancestral temples.[8]

Archaeological excavations carried on both at Hou-chia-chuang
and Hsiao-t'un have brought to light post-Shang burials as well
as evidences of post-Shang occupation, although to a greatly re-

[7]What really took place during the battle of conquest of the Shang by the
Chou is still preserved in some documents, such as certain chapters of *I Chou
Shu* (in Chinese) (Ssu-pu-ts'ung-k'an edition [Shanghai, 1919–1929]); chap.
xxxvi on "Conquering Yin," and chap. xl on "Captives" throw a great deal of
light on this famous battle.

[8]Édouard Chavannes, *Les Mémoires historiques de Se-Ma-Ts'ien* (Paris,
1895–1906), IV, chap. xxxviii, "Le Vicomte de Wei, (Prince de) Song,"
230–31.

duced extent. It is clear at any rate that Hsiao-t'un was abandoned gradually and converted to agricultural land only a part at a time.

Thus there have been discovered enough criteria by means of which the archaeological remains of Hsiao-t'un may be divided into four substages: (1) the premetallic substage of the Black Pottery culture; (2) the predynastic substage of the Shang culture; (3) the dynastic Shang culture; and (4) the post-Shang substage. The lines of division that mark the various substages are in most cases stratigraphically definite and chronologically under control. They may be arranged in tabular form as shown in Table 1.

The major portion of the bronze collection made at Hou-chia-chuang and Hsiao-t'un belongs to the *hang-t'u* period (Hsiao-t'un 3); some pieces are assignable to Hsiao-t'un 2. A few pieces may be as late as Hsiao-t'un 4. Those which follow Hsiao-t'un 4 were the finds of the Western Chou dynasty and their sequels.

ANALYSES

Eight samples of Hsiao-t'un bronzes were analyzed in 1947 by the National Research Institute of Chemistry at the request of the Archaeological Section; the results are arranged in Table 2.

The detailed percentages of the component minerals shown in Table 2 may be roughly divided into three groups: specimens 3 and 6, each with more than 90 per cent of the element copper, form one group; specimen 1, with a relatively large proportion of lead, forms a group by itself; then the remaining five specimens, each containing more than 10 per cent of the element tin, form the third group. The last group is comprised entirely of vessels of the ceremonial type, while groups 1 and 2 are specimens of tools and weapons. I have in my possession a series of analyses of the *ko* halbert of different periods; Table 3 shows the results of the various analyses. It is revealing to compare the chemical compositions of the *ko* halberts of the various periods. The increasing

TABLE 2

CHEMICAL ANALYSES OF BRONZE SPECIMENS EXCAVATED FROM HSIAO-T'UN

Sample Number	Type of Specimen	Sn	Pb	Cu	Fe	Zn	Ni	Total (%)
3.	Arrow-head	1.83	1.85	96.06	0.03	no trace	not determined	99.77
6.	Knife handle	3.67	1.03	94.65	0.05	no trace	not determined	99.40
1.	Ko blade	4.01	2.59	88.98	0.13	no trace	not determined	95.71
2.	Upright vessel	13.07	0.83	83.73	0.04	no trace	not determined	97.67
4.	Décor piece	16.27	0.22	80.25	0.12	no trace	not determined	96.86
8.	Décor piece	16.78	0.06	82.99	0.05	no trace	not determined	99.88
7.	Edge of vessel	17.65	0.09	81.74	0.06	no trace	not determined	99.54
5.	Vessel piece	20.32	0.05	79.12	0.04	no trace	not determined	99.53

TABLE 3

CHEMICAL ANALYSES OF FIVE KO SPECIMENS FROM THREE LOCALITIES: ANYANG, CHÜN HSIEN, AND CHI HSIEN

Sample* Number	Localities	Sn	Pb	Cu	Fe	Zn	Ni	Total (%)
HT. 1	E16(1634)	4.01	2.59	88.98	0.13	no trace	not determined	95.71
HTs. 3	M28.8	13.61	0.78	82.72	0.05	0.10	not determined	97.26
HTs. 4	M29.8	10.75	0.10	87.44	0.10	0.09	not determined	98.48
HTs. 5	M19.2	12.10	12.41	73.38	0.11	0.07	not determined	98.07
SPT. 7	73	17.61	13.55	66.27	0.22	0.13	0.11	97.89

* HT. 1: Shang dynasty; HTs. 3, 4, 5: Western Chou dynasty; SPT. 7: Eastern Chou dynasty.

proportions of the tin and the lead elements in the later periods serve to indicate some significant change in the supply of these two minerals. In the Chou dynasty tremendous new activities might have prevailed in the search for new sources of these minerals, and, as a result, their supply might have been much more abundant to the people of northern Honan. The copper supply seems never to have worried the Bronze Age people of this area since the Shang dynasty. Old gazetteers recorded many copper mines in this region; a recent compilation of these records[9] shows that, within a radius of 300 kilometers of Anyang, no fewer than nineteen copper mines were mentioned. The one at Yuan-chü, less than 300 kilometers from the ancient remains of the Shang capital, was still a great center for money coinage in the Northern Sung dynasty. The mineral specimens from this district, collected in 1948, were on exhibition in the Geological Survey in Nanking.

Such data as the above fit into the historical conditions of the Shang dynasty very well; otherwise, it would be difficult to explain the intense activity and the great output of the bronze products of this period. But the low proportions of the tin and lead found in the making of the *ko* halbert during the Shang dynasty cannot be satisfactorily explained by merely resorting to the interpretation that the supply of these raw materials was limited; as a matter of fact, these two minerals were quite generously provided in the casting of ceremonial vessels (see Table 2).

Moreover, the *ko* halbert is not the only type of specimen whose composition shows a low percentage of tin. The arrowhead and the knife handle, as analyzed in the above table, also contained a low proportion of this mineral. Thus it seems that, as early as the Shang time, there was already a distinct correlation between the type of product and the relative proportion of different minerals that entered into the composition of the alloy. On the basis of

[9]Motonosuke Amano, "Mining and Agriculture in the Yin Dynasty," *Tôhô Gakuhô (Journal of Oriental Studies)* (Kyoto), No. 23 (1953), p. 236.

such distinctions found among the compositions of the alloys of different bronze articles, it is even justifiable to indulge to a certain extent in some speculation as to whether some of the products might have appeared earlier than others.

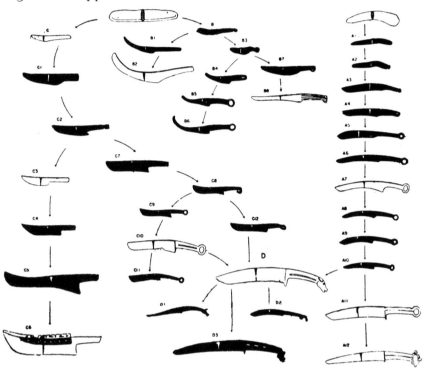

FIG. 7. *Structural relations of different types of bronze knives excavated from Hsiao-t'un and Hou-chia-chuang. (Reproduced from "Studies of Hsiao-t'un Bronzes, Part II," by Li Chi, in Chinese Journal of Archaeology, Vol. IV [1949], fig. 26)*

Evidence is not lacking to indicate that bronze knives dug out from pits underlying the pisé foundation might have been manufactured in an earlier period. The one mentioned in my article of 1948 (see note 11) is a case that illustrates the point. The pit in which this knife was found is YH379 and is located in the excavation unit C333. Directly above this pit was the *hang-t'u* stratum (夯土) gamma 16. The convex-edged knife (Pl. XII, 2) is unique

49

among the Hsiao-t'un finds and does not seem to have reappeared in the *hang-t'u* period. While the pit YH379 might be of the Shang period, judging by its general contents, the possibility of the presence of some early survival in such a definitely stratified pit is certainly greater than in pits without so distinctive a position. Another distinctive attribute of this find is the method of its casting by a one-piece mold, with only one side in relief and the other side entirely flat. At a later period, namely the *hang-t'u* stage, symmetrical knives (Pl. XII, 3–9) with similar reliefs on both sides were manufactured. To achieve this purpose, valve molds were undoubtedly used. Whether the method of using the internal molds was introduced at the same time it is difficult to say. In my article referred to above, I divided the nineteen specimens of bronze knives from Hsiao-t'un into three types according to the methods by which they were manufactured: (1) single-mold casting, articles with one side flat, two samples; (2) valve-mold casting, articles symmetrical on both sides, thirteen specimens; (3) multimold casting with the occasional employment of internal molds, four specimens (Pl. XII, 8, 9). It is important to point out that all the nineteen specimens of the bronze knives from Hsiao-t'un were designed for daily use; in no case were they made for burial purposes, as is true of many of the Hou-chia-chuang knives (Fig. 7).

MOLDS

In this connection it may be fitting to say a few words about the molds excavated from Hsiao-t'un. The collection of these artifacts reached quite a respectable size after the fifteenth season in Anyang. Most of the better preserved pieces, that is, those with patterns still distinctly shown, are light gray in color, occasionally mixed with a light brownish hue, and they are more or less porous in composition. The back part of the mold is usually irregular, and the edges, if not broken, are tenoned or mortised in many cases. Many of these fragments are complete and have suffered no damage as far as external appearances are concerned, but no success has been achieved in attempts to piece the individual fragments together into a complete unit originally used in the casting operation.

It is also remarkable that, while hundreds of clay molds were collected, not a single piece of stone mold was found. There are many pieces of stone carvings in the Academia Sinica collection, but none of them could have served as a model for these clay negatives. On the other hand, a number of clay models (Pl. XIII) were discovered; they were evidently molded after the shape of the article in the process of being cast, and on them the molds that were to serve as negatives for direct casting were to be printed. On these models, decorative patterns in relief were worked out just as one finds them on the finished products in bronzes; in several cases, on the relieved parts, fine lines were drawn in red or black pigments (Pl. XIII, upper right), which were evidently to be incised afterward. These half-finished models discovered at Hsiao-t'un throw a great deal of light on the early history of bronze casting.

Most of the clay molds were well baked; some attained a degree of hardness almost comparable with that of stoneware. It is interesting to note that one of the hard-baked pieces was incised with a character (Pl. XIV, 2) not yet decipherable but obviously the name of a person whose property this mold might have been. As the character was incised on the back part of the mold, it could not have been intended for casting. So, if the incised character was for the purpose of identification, the object to be identified would be the mold itself rather than the article to be cast after this mold.

Several fragments for casting arrowheads were found (Pl. XIV, 5). They belong evidently to the valve type; no molds so simple that they might have been used for the open-hearth process were discovered. Inner molds were found in abundance—a definite indication that the foundry at Hsiao-t'un in the Shang time was a factory for the production of an advanced type of bronze. The factory was well supplied with plenty of malachite and prepared ingots of imported tin. Both these minerals were discovered during our excavations.[10]

SHAPES

In my first study of the Hsiao-t'un bronzes,[11] I listed eighty-two specimens of the containers, including six covers, which were excavated from this site. Covers excepted, the seventy-six containers were divisible into five classes: round-bottomed, flat-based, ring-footed, tripod, and tetrapod; these five classes were again divided into nineteen types. Tools and weapons were studied in my second article.[12] There are eighty-one specimens within this category besides arrowheads, and they are divided into four classes and fourteen types. Chariot parts, ornamental pieces, and articles of miscellaneous character which do not belong to the first two categories still remain unclassified, since most of them were parts of, or attached to, composite tools, weapons, or chariots. They will be discussed in relation to the things which they decorate or of which they constitute a part. Bronzes in the Hou-chia-chuang collection are amazingly similar to those from Hsiao-t'un, but they are richer in variety of forms, bigger in size, and better made. Owing to the highly dilapidated conditions in both sites, it is difficult to say whether the differences found so far are more

[10]Liu Yü-hsia, "Study of the Bronze Casting Technique of the Yin Dynasty," *Preliminary Reports of Excavations at Anyang* (in Chinese), Part IV (1933), pp. 681–96.

[11]Li Chi, "Studies of Hsiao-t'un Bronzes, Part I," *Chinese Journal of Archaeology* (in Chinese), III (1948), 1–93.

[12]Li Chi, "Studies of Hsiao-t'un Bronzes, Part II," *Chinese Journal of Archaeology* (in Chinese), IV (1949), 1–70.

apparent than real. About their contemporaneity there seems to be hardly any doubt.

Among the Hou-chia-chuang bronzes there were certain pieces (Pl. XV) that were never duplicated in the Hsiao-t'un collection; but the majority of the bronze forms are about the same, and many of the specimens from these two sites could be exchanged without being recognized. So, on the whole, it is safe to say that the two collections are the products of the same period, and that whatever marks the Hou-chia-chuang group off is mainly due to the custom that the best bronzes went to the royal tombs.[13]

The shapes of most of the containers found in Hsiao-t'un could be accounted for. The tetrapods, tripods, and ring-foots as well as the flat-based containers evidently derived their forms from the wooden and the pottery receptacles. Tools and weapons found their prototypes in implements made of bone, stone, or antlers. There are also a number of articles whose origins are obscure. One of the Hsiao-t'un flat-based specimens is a pan-shaped bronze, originally found in broken condition in YM331. Restored, it looks very much like a frying pan, with a big rim whose diameter

[13]The term "royal tombs," as far as I am aware, was first employed by Professor Paul Pelliot in his lecture at Harvard University on the occasion of its tercentenary celebration (see "The Royal Tombs of Anyang," in *Independence, Convergence and Borrowing in Institution, Thought and Art* [Cambridge, Mass.: Harvard University Press, 1937], pp. 265–72]; the field archaeologist who worked in Hou-chia-chuang called them simply big tombs and small tombs. Liang Ssu-yung, Director of the Hou-chia-chuang excavations, labeled the map of this cemetery area as "Thousand Tombs Cemetery Area of Hou-chia-chuang." But there is much justification for Professor Pelliot's adoption of this descriptive term. Tomb HPKM:1001, for instance, as surveyed, shows a total content of no less than 4,200 cubic meters; so, to dig the pit alone, it must have required no less than 4,200 day-labor units, if one labor unit at that time could have removed one cubic meter of dirt in a day, as the best of farm hands nowadays, with a much superior tool and better incentive, might occasionally be able to do. It is scarcely imaginable that in the neighborhood of the capital of the ruling dynasty any other group of people, aside from the royal clan, were in the position to command such wealth and power.

measures 52 cm.[14] It is undoubtedly the forerunner of the frying pan used by every Chinese housewife, but its origin is rather indefinite.

If these two collections are taken as typical Shang dynasty bronzes and compared with the Hsin-ts'un collection of the Western Chou and the Shan-piao-chen collection of the Eastern Chou time, certain marked changes in the shapes of the containers are evident. In the post-Shang periods the tetrapod class almost completely disappeared while the tripod class persisted but had undergone a great number of structural modifications.[15] The *ting* tripods of the Eastern Chou periods acquired covers, and the *hsien* steamer was cast in two pieces in the Eastern Chou. A number of new shapes made their appearance in the later periods, owing partly to changes of customs as well as to technical improvements. The best group of bronzes that may be taken to illustrate such changes are the *ko* halberts, which were found all through the Bronze Age of China and were represented by a large number of examples in all the above collections.

The *ko* halbert is a weapon used for more than one thousand years by the Chinese fighting force in the classical period. It is a typical Chinese invention and developed exclusively in China. In 1950, the *Bulletin of the Institute of History and Philology* published my article on "Typological Studies of the Bronze Kou-ping (Chinese Halberts) Excavated from Northern Honan, with a Classified and Illustrated List." In this article the development of *ko*, leading gradually from the stone prototype and bronze imitation, through the various intermediate stages to the ideal shape as laid down in the famous version of "K'ao Kung Chi," was

[14]See Li Chi, "Studies of Hsiao-t'un Bronzes, Part I," p. 68.

[15]Kuo Pao-chün, "Preliminary Report on the Excavations of the Ancient Cemetery at Hsin-ts'un, Chün Hsien, Honan," *T'ien-yeh-k'ao-ku-pao-kao* (in Chinese), No. 1 (Shanghai, 1936), pp. 167–200.

traced.[16] The specimens examined are 208 in number and belong to the following five collections:

Collection	Specimens
1. Hsiao-t'un	35
2. Hou-chia-chuang	31
3. Hsin-ts'un	67
4. Shan-piao-chen[17]	59
5. Liu-li-ko	16
Total	208

The first two groups belong to the Shang dynasty; the Hsin-ts'un collection consists mainly of remains of the Western Chou time; while the fourth and the fifth groups represent the period of the Warring States. The typological characteristics of these three periods may be summarized in the following terms.

1. The *ko* of the Shang dynasty is of the simplest type (Pls. XVI, XVII); it is frequently composed of an elongated tongue-shaped blade made of jade or other hard stone of fine grain, which may be hafted into a T-shaped bronze sleeve (Pl. XVII, 7). A more primitive type of *ko* (Pl. XX, 1–3), evidently of early survival and used exclusively for burials, is made completely of stone; it is merely an elongated blade, pointed at one end, and with the other end cut into a tang for hafting. All-bronze *ko* of this period were usually cast in imitation of the jade-with-bronze-sleeve type; the two projecting points on both edges of the socket were retained at the junction between the blade (*yuan*) and the hafting part (*nei*). These structural peculiarities were never found in the stone prototype.

[16]"K'ao Kung Chi" (the artificers' record) is a section of the *Chou Li*, one of the Thirteen Classics. There is a French translation, *Le Tcheou-li*, by Édouard Biot (Paris, 1851).

[17]The excavations at Shan-piao-chen and Liu-li-ko are not yet reported.

Stone *ko* were found in large numbers in both Hou-chia-chuang and Hsiao-t'un. It is interesting to note that in one of the Hou-chia-chuang royal tombs (HPKM: 1001), together with the underground guards buried in the sacrificial pits underneath the wooden chamber, there was found in each case a *ko* halbert. The one found in the central pit, evidently the resting place of the chief guard and much larger in size than the other pits (Pl. IV), is made entirely of stone; those found in the corner pits are all made of bronze. There is no doubt here that the weapon made of stone was given a more honored position chiefly for its greater antiquity.

2. In the Western Chou period, both the inventive genius of the founders and the innate qualities of the metallic substance began to assert themselves, and the results were expressed in the new types of *ko* halberts (Pl. XVIII) which were evolved from a more primitive form found in the preceding dynasty. In this period there is, for the first time, a definite sign of the development of *hu* (胡), or necking, namely, a downward projection at the hafting section of the blade; it was, no doubt, a device invented by the foundry master to improve the efficiency of hafting. The continuous development of *hu*, mainly its projection downward, took place in this period. In the Hsin-ts'un collection the variation of this particular feature is most noticeable. As the different specimens show, a number of ingenious experiments were made for the purpose of increasing the efficiency of this

FIG. 8. *Ink rubbing of the decorative pattern of a chien basin from Shan-piao-chen, Chi Hsien*

weapon. There was an effort made, for instance, to combine the *ko* and the *mao* (矛) into one composite weapon, an experiment which did not achieve any success till several hundred years later (Fig. 8).

3. The typological development of the *ko* reached its zenith in the period of the Warring States (Pl. XIX). The classical description of the standard type of *ko* (Pl. XX, 4) provided by "K'ao Kung Chi" was a product of this period. In the *ko* of this period, not only was the hafting process perfected but ingenious use was also made of the originally useless *nei*. In the earlier time the *nei* had served only ornamental purposes, but it was now put

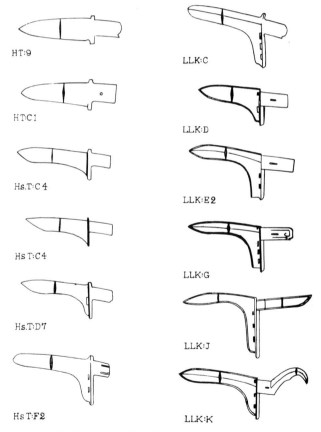

HT:9

HT:C1

Hs.T:C4

Hs T:C4

Hs.T:D7

Hs T:F2

LLK:C

LLK:D

LLK:E2

LLK:G

LLK:J

LLK:K

FIG. 9. *Typological evolution of the ko halbert*

to effective use by being provided with sharp points and edges or sometimes bent into hook-shaped cutters (Pl. XIX, 5, 10). A device was finally found, after a long series of experiments, to combine effectively the *ko* and the *mao*, namely, the halbert and the spearhead, into one effective weapon, the *chi* (戟) (Fig. 8), with which the State of Ch'in unified China for the first time. It was with this same weapon that the Emperor Han Wu-ti subdued his rivals in both Central and Eastern Asia.

These three typological stages are all well illustrated by the five collections mentioned above (Fig. 9). In the period of the Warring States, iron was already in use for making agricultural implements. At exactly what time bronze was fully replaced by iron in the manufacture of weapons is, archaeologically speaking, still

TABLE 4
BRONZE AGE OF CHINA

Period	Type Site	Characteristic Features	Chronology
Early Bronze	Hsiao-t'un 2 (YH379) (Anyang)	Open-hearth casting Knives with one side flat	Predynastic Shang
Middle Bronze I	Hsiao-t'un 3 (E16) Hou-chia-chuang royal tombs (Anyang)	Valve molds and internal molds Simple-bladed *ko* Big bronze vessels	Dynastic Shang ca. (1384–1111 B.C.)
Middle Bronze II	Hsin-ts'un tombs (Chün Hsien)	Method of casting same as above Curved-bladed *ko* with developing *hu* Tetrapods disappeared	Western Chou
Late Bronze	Shan-piao-chen tombs (Chi Hsien) Liu-li-ko tombs (Hui Hsien)	*Ko* of "K'ao Kung Chi" type with sharpened *nei* Chi (戟)	Eastern Chou

uncertain. What is definite is that the evolution of the *ko* halbert must have taken nearly one thousand years before it reached its perfection, and its active service must have lasted more than a millennium before it was finally abandoned. The various stages of the typological development of this weapon have a chronological value which can hardly be equaled by any other group of artifacts of the Bronze Age. But to trace back to the earliest stage and the origin of this era, there is still a great deal of work that must be done. The data selected for the present survey were all collected by our own field workers from the northern part of Honan. There are many key areas equally important for archaeological purposes but totally unknown. Until these areas have been examined with scientific care, it would be rash indeed to postulate a definite theory about the origin of the Chinese Bronze Age.

Plates

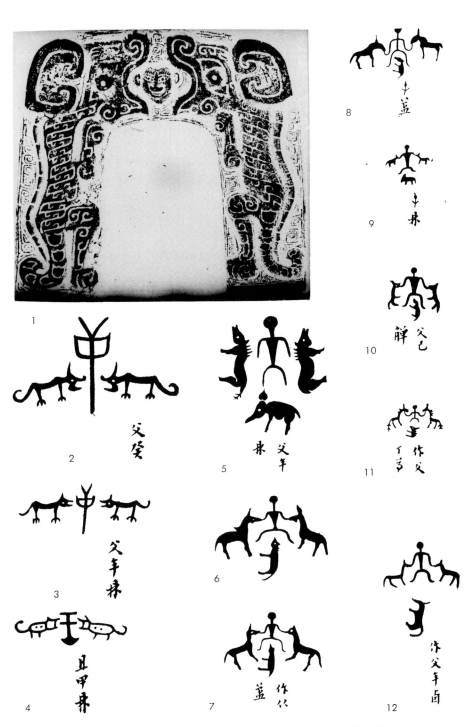

PLATE I. 1, *Ink rubbing of the decorative pattern on the standing lug above the rim of a tetrapod discovered in the neighborhood of Hou-chia-chuang; 2–12, bronze inscriptions from Jung Keng's Chin-wen-pien (Inscriptions on Bronzes) (2nd ed. rev. and enl.; Ch'ang-sha, 1939), supplementary chapter, p. 26.*

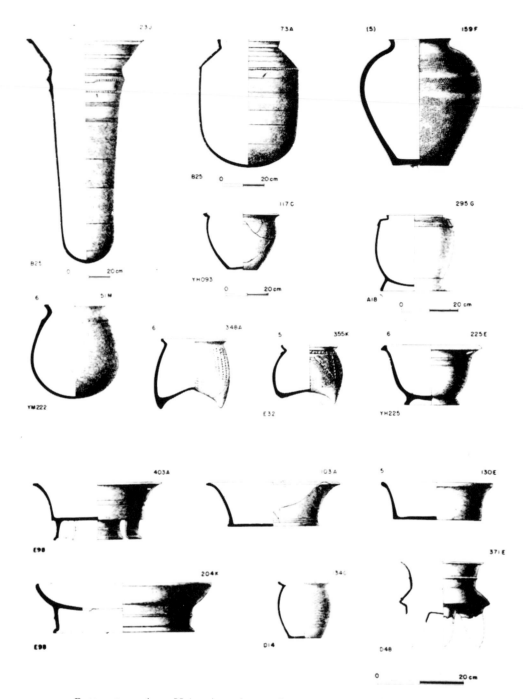

PLATE II. *Pottery types from Hsiao-t'un: above, nine common types from the Shang stratum; below, six common types from the pre-Shang stratum*

PLATE III. Fragments of human figures in stone: left, from Hou-chia-chuang; right, from Hsiao-t'un

PLATE IV. *Floor of the wooden chamber of HPKM:1001, Hou-chia-chuang*

PLATE V. *Drum and musical stone discovered together with remnants of their hanging frames in HPKM:1217, Hou-chia-chuang*

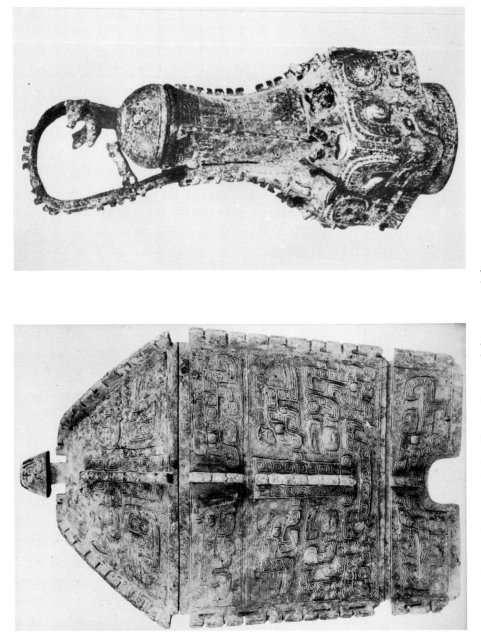

PLATE VI. *Square bronzes of the Shang dynasty: left, square yi from Hou-chia-chuang; right, square yu from Hsiao-t'un*

PLATE VII. Left, ting tripod from Hsiao-t'un; right, ku from Hsiao-t'un

PLATE VIII. *Two types of bronze decorations from Hou-chia-chuang: above, tzu decorated with animal patterns; below, tzu decorated with spirals only*

PLATE IX. Above, p'an from Hou-chia-chuang with geometrical patterns; below, yü from Hou-chia-chuang with animal patterns

PLATE X. *Tin ingots from Hsiao-t'un*

PLATE XI. Building foundations of stamped earth, discovered at Hsiao-t'un: above, earth floor of a Shang dynasty house; below, side view of the structure of the stamped earth, 20 layers in succession

PLATE XII. Types of bronze knives excavated from Hsiao-t'un and Hou-chia-chuang: 1, 2, one-sided flat knives; 3–7, symmetrical shapes, showing bivalve casting; 8, 9, hollowed handles, indicating use of internal mold

PLATE XIII. Clay models for casting in bronze, all from Hsiao-t'un. Specimen upper right still retains traces of lines drawn in red pigment

PLATE XIV. Clay molds used for casting bronzes, from Hsiao-t'un: 1, 4, clay negatives for socketed spear handles; 5, mold for casting arrowheads; 2, 3, 6, molds with signs

PLATE XV. Ting tripod with a big handle, from Hou-chia-chuang

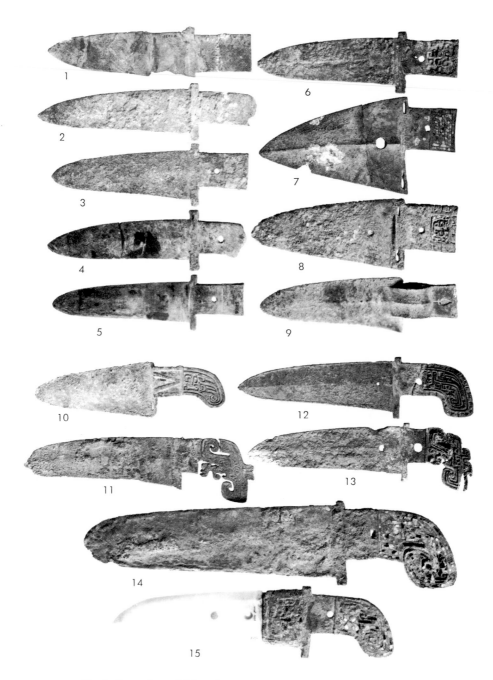

PLATE XVI. *Ko halberts from Hsiao-t'un*

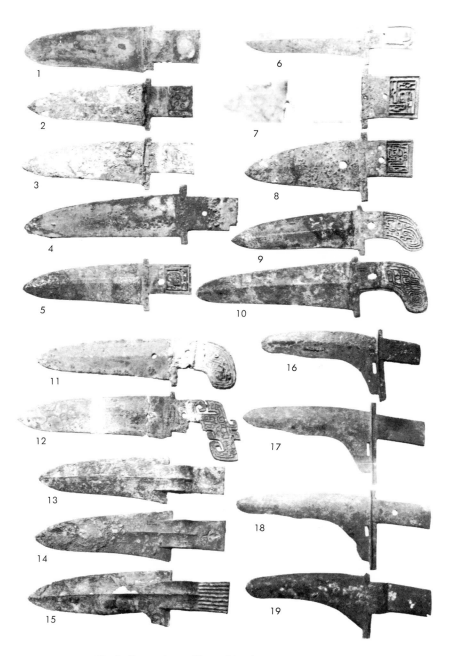

PLATE XVII. Ko halberts from Hou-chia-chuang

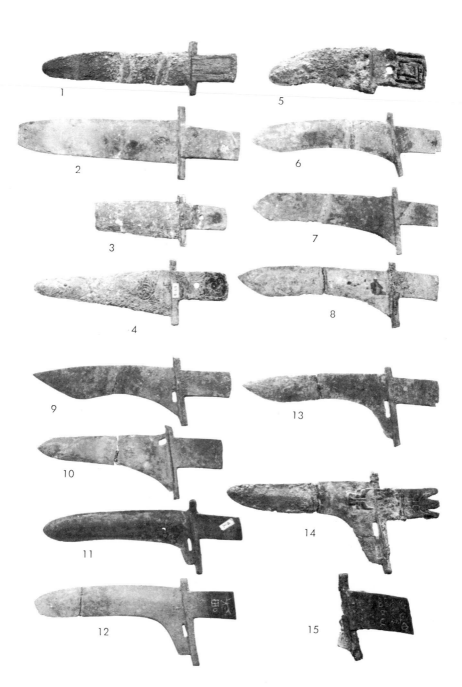

PLATE XVIII. Ko halberts from Hsin-ts'un, Chün Hsien

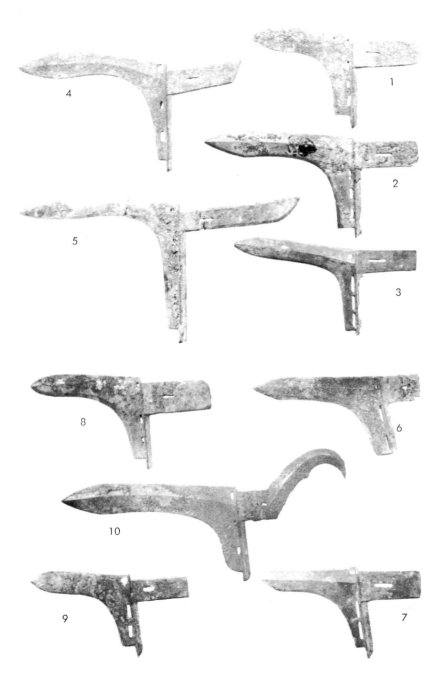

PLATE XIX. Ko halberts from Liu-li-kuo, Hui Hsien

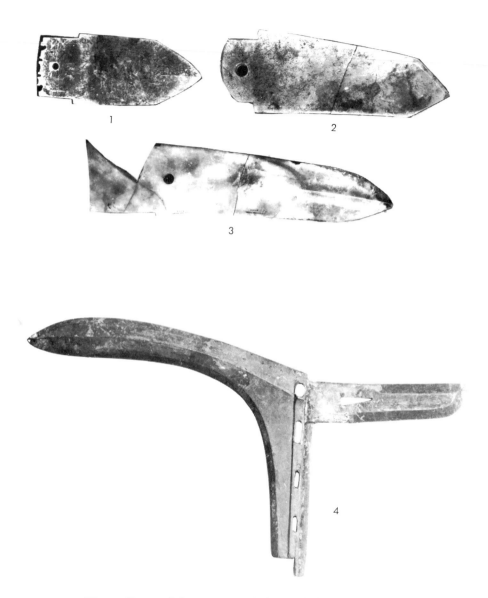

PLATE XX. The earliest and latest types of the ko halbert: 1–3, stone ko from Hou-chia-chuang, Shang dynasty; 4, bronze ko from Ch'ang-sa, Chan-kuo period

Supplementary Plates

The following supplementary plates have been chosen to illustrate further and more extensively the art works of the Shang dynasty as expressed in the media of stone and bronze and discussed in Lectures II and III. The stone carvings were all excavated from the Hou-chia-chuang cemetery site; most of the marbles used for these sculptures came from the local quarries located within a radius of less than twenty miles from the cemetery. The Hsiao-t'un bronzes have all been described in "Studies of Hsiao-t'un Bronzes, Part I," by Li Chi, in the *Chinese Journal of Archaeology*, Vol. III (1948). The two big *chi* tetrapods from Hou-chia-chuang are the largest bronzes discovered by the field workers of Academia Sinica since scientific digging started in North China.

Plates XXI–XXX. Stone carvings showing the various phases of animal styles developed in the dynastic Shang period, all excavated from Hou-chia-chuang. HPKM is an abbreviation for "Hsi-pei-kang one thousand tombs"; the number following is the individual tomb number.

Plates XXXI–L. Types of Shang bronzes of the dynastic period excavated from Hsiao-t'un (HT) and Hou-chia-chuang (HCC). YM is an abbreviation for Yin Mu; HPKM is an abbreviation for "Hsi-pei-kang one thousand tombs"; the number following is the individual tomb number.

PLATE XXI. *Oxhead, marble. HPKM:1001. Length, 29.2 cm.*

PLATE XXII. *Eagle-headed monster, marble.* HPKM:1001. Length, 34.0 cm.

PLATE XXIII. *Tiger-headed monster, marble. HPKM:1001. Length,*
37.0 cm.

PLATE XXIV. *Double-faced monster with incurved trunks, marble.*
HPKM:1001. Height, 18.9 cm.

PLATE XXV. *Frog, limestone. HPKM:1001. Length, 12.5 cm.*

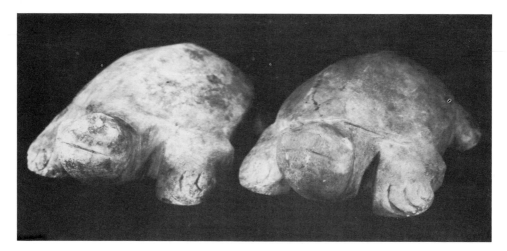

PLATE XXVI. *Two turtles, limestone. HPKM:1001. Left, length, 16.5 cm.; right, length, 16.9 cm.*

PLATE XXVII. *Oblong block in the shape of two froglike monsters with hind parts joined, marble. HPKM:1001. Length, 84.0 cm.*

PLATE XXVIII. *Elephant, jade.* HPKM:1567. Length, 27.0 cm.

PLATE XXIX. *Buffalo, marble.* HPKM:1500. Length, 27.5 cm.

PLATE XXX. *Three tiger pendants. Top, HPKM:2045, length, 8.3 cm.; middle, HPKM:2004, length, 9.1 cm.; bottom, HPKM:2004, length, 8.6 cm.*

PLATE XXXI. *Ku vase. YM:331 (HT).*
Height, 18.6 cm.

PLATE XXXII. Ku vase. YM:331 (HT).
Height, 19.4 cm.

PLATE XXXIII. Tsun vessel. YM:331 (HT). Height, 34.1 cm.

PLATE XXXIV. Pu flask. YM:331 (HT). Height, 24.1 cm.

PLATE XXXV. Pu flask. YM:232 (HT). Height, 24.9 cm.

PLATE XXXVI. Pu flask. YM:188 (HT). Height, 15.4 cm.

PLATE XXXVII. *Yi vessel, square.* YM:288
(HT). *Height, 16.2 cm.*

PLATE XXXVIII. *Yu bottle, square.* YM:331
(HT). Height, including cover, 30.3 cm.
See also Plate VI, right

PLATE XXXIX. Yu *bottle*, round. HPKM:
1022 *(HCC)*. Height, including cover,
25.0 cm.

PLATE XL. Ting tripod. YM:333 (HT).
Height, up to rim, 10.5 cm.

PLATE XLI. Li-ting tripod. YM:388 (HT). Height, up to rim, 16.5 cm.

PLATE XLII. Ting tripod. YM:331 (HT).
Height, up to rim, 11.0 cm.

PLATE XLIII. Hsien tripod. YM:188 (HT). Height, up to rim, 47.2 cm.

PLATE XLIV. Hsien tripod. YM:331 (HT).
Height, up to rim, 35.1 cm.

PLATE XLV. Hu tripod. YM:331 (HT).
Height, up to rim, 18.3 cm.

PLATE XLVI. Chia tripod. YM:188 (HT).
Height, up to rim, 32.0 cm.

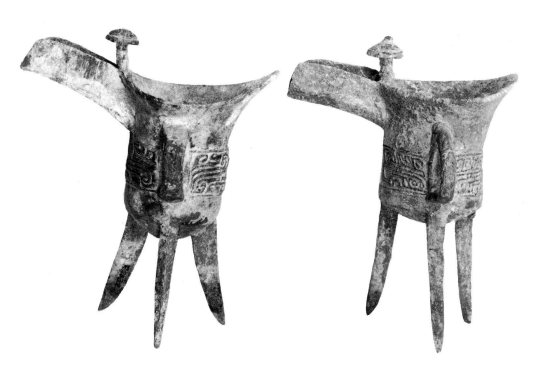

PLATE XLVII. *Two tsueh tripods. Left, YM:329 (HT), height, up to rim, 13.9 cm.; right, YM:388 (HT), height, up to rim, 14.0 cm. Unlike most tsueh, these two vessels have only one, instead of two, vertical projections at the base of the spout*

PLATE XLVIII. *Two tsueh tripods. Left, YM:308 (HT), height, up to rim, 17.3 cm.; right, YM:238 (HT), height, up to rim, 18.3 cm.*

PLATE XLIX. Chi tetrapod. HPKM:1004 (HCC). Height, up to rim, 74.0 cm.

PLATE L. Chi *tetrapod. HPKM:1004 (HCC). Height, up to rim, 62.0 cm.*

Bibliography

Amano, Motonosuke. "Mining and Agriculture in the Yin Dynasty," *Tôhô Gakuhô* (*Journal of Oriental Studies*) (Kyoto), No. 23 (1953).

Andersson, J. G. "Researches into the Prehistory of the Chinese," *Bulletin of the Museum of Far Eastern Antiquities* (Stockholm), No. 15 (1943).

Biot, Édouard (trans.). *Le Tcheou-li* [*Chou Li*]; ou, *Rites des Tcheou*. 3 vols. in 2. Paris: Imprimerie nationale, 1851.

Black, Davidson. "On the Human Skeletal Remains from Yangshao Ts'un in Comparison with Recent North China Skeletal Materials," *Palaeontologia Sinica*, Ser. D, Vol. I, Fasc. 3 (1925).

———. "A Study of Kansu and Honan Aëneolithic Skulls and Specimens from Later Kansu Prehistoric Sites in Comparison with North China and Other Recent Crania," *Palaeontologia Sinica*, Ser. D, Vol. VI, Fasc. 1 (1928).

Boas, Franz. *Primitive Art*. Oslo: H. Aschehoug & Co., 1927.

113

Bibliography

*Chang, Kwang-chih. "Notes on Some Anthropometrical Measurements of the Freshmen of the National Taiwan University," *Bulletin of the Department of Archaeology and Anthropology*, No. 3 (1954), pp. 39–50.

Chavannes, Édouard. *La Sculpture sur pierre en Chine au temps des deux dynasties Han.* Paris: E. Leroux, 1893.

———. *Les Mémoires historiques de Se-Ma-Ts'ien.* Paris: E. Leroux, 1895–1905.

Childe, V. Gordon. *New Light on the Most Ancient East.* New York: Frederick A. Praeger Inc., 1952.

Dubs, Homer H. *Works of Hsüntze.* (Probsthain's Oriental Series, Vol. XVI.) London, 1928.

———. "The Date of the Shang Period," *T'oung Pao*, XL, Nos. 4–5 (1951), 322–35.

Frankfort, Henri. *The Birth of Civilization in the Near East.* London: Williams & Norgate, 1951.

*Fu, Ssu-nien. "Aim and Method of the Works of the National Research Institute of History and Philology," *Bulletin of the National Research Institute of History and Philology of the Academia Sinica*, I, No. 1 (1928), 3–10.

*———. *Collected Papers of Fu Meng-chen*, Vol. IV. Taipei: National Taiwan University, 1952.

Hooton, E. A. *Up from the Ape.* Rev. ed. New York: Macmillan, 1946.

*Hsia, Nai. "New Discoveries of a Ch'i Chia Culture," *Chinese Journal of Archaeology*, III (1948), 101–17.

*Hu, Hou-hsüan. "Agricultural Records of the Yin Dynasty from the Oracle Bone Inscriptions," *Chia Ku Hsüeh Shang Shih Lun Ts'ung*, Vol. II (1945).

Hummel, A. W. *The Autobiography of a Chinese Historian.* (Sinica Leidensia Series.) Leiden: E. J. Brill, 1931. (Translation of the preface of *Ku-shih-pien* by Ku Chieh-kang.)

*I Chou Shu. Ssu-pu-ts'ung-k'an edition. Shanghai, 1919–29.

*Jung, Keng. *Photographic Reproductions of the Rubbings of the Tomb Figures of Wu Liang Tz'u.* Monograph No. 3, Yenching Archaeological Society, 1934.

*———. *Chin-wen-pien (Inscriptions on Bronzes).* 2nd ed., rev. and enl. Ch'ang-sha, 1939.

Kanazeki, T., S. Miyake, and S. Mizuno. "Yang Teon-Wa," *Archaeologia Orientalis*, Ser. B, Vol. III (1942).

Koop, Albert J. *Early Chinese Bronzes.* London: E. Benn, Ltd., 1924.

*In Chinese.

114

*Ku, Chieh-kang. *Ku-shih-pien*, Vol. I (1926). (See Hummel, A. W.)

*Kuo, Pao-chün. "Preliminary Report on the Excavations of the Ancient Cemetery at Hsin Ts'un, Chün Hsien, Honan," *T'ien-yeh-k'ao-ku-pao-kao*, No. 1 (Shanghai, 1936), pp. 167–200.

Legge, James (trans.). *Ch'un Ts'ew [Ch'un Ch'iu]*. (The Chinese Classics series, Vol. V, Part I.) Hongkong: Lane Crawford & Co.; London: Trübner & Co., 1872.

——— (trans.). *Li Chi*. Thirteen Classics edition, Vol. XII. (In Part III of *The Sacred Books of China*, translated by James Legge, in the series The Sacred Books of the East, edited by F. Max Müller, Vol. XXVII.) Oxford, 1885.

*Li, Chi. "Recent Excavations at Anyang and a Summary of Six Seasons' Works (1929–1932)," *Preliminary Reports of Excavations at Anyang*, Part IV (Peking and Nanking, 1933), pp. 559–78.

*———. "Pre-Yin Cultural Deposits under the Surface of Hsiao-t'un," *Hsüeh Shu Hui K'an* (Chungkung, published by Academia Sinica), No. 1 (1944), pp. 1–14.

*———. "Studies of Hsiao-t'un Bronzes, Part I," *Chinese Journal of Archaeology*, III (1948), 1–100.

*———. "Studies of Hsiao-t'un Bronzes, Part II," *Bulletin of the College of Arts* (National Taiwan University), No. 4 (1949), pp. 179–240. Also *Chinese Journal of Archaeology*, IV (1949), 1–70.

*———. "Typological Studies of the Bronze Kou-ping (Chinese Halberts) Excavated from Northern Honan, with a Classified and Illustrated List," *Bulletin of the Institute of History and Philology*, XXII (1950), 1–18.

*———. "Chemical Analyses of Different Types of Hsiao-t'un Potteries," in *Memorial Volume of President Fu Ssu-nien*. Taipei: National Taiwan University, 1952.

———. "Diverse Background of the Decorative Art of the Shang Dynasty," *Proceedings of the Eighth Pacific Science Congress*, I (Quezon City, Philippines, 1955), 179–94.

———, et al. (eds.). *Ch'eng-tzu-yai: The Black Pottery Culture Site at Lung-shan-chen in Li-ch'eng-hsien, Shantung Province*. Translation by Kenneth Starr of *Archaeologia Sinica*, No. 1 (1934). (Yale Publications in Anthropology, 52.) New Haven: Yale University Press, 1956.

*Liang, Ssu-yung. "Preliminary Report on the Excavation at Hou-kang," *Preliminary Reports of Excavations at Anyang*, Part IV (Peking and Nanking, 1933), pp. 609–26.

*In Chinese.

Bibliography

*———. *Ch'eng-tzu-yai*. English summary. Nanking, 1934. (See also under Li, Chi, *et al*. [eds.].)

———. "The Lungshan Culture, a Prehistoric Phase of Chinese Civilization," *Proceedings of the Sixth Pacific Science Congress*, IV (1939), 59–79.

*Licent, E., P. Teilhard de Chardin, and Davidson Black. "On a Presumably Pleistocene Human Tooth from the Sjara-osso-gol Deposit," *Bulletin of the Geological Society of China*, V, No. 1 (1926), 285–90.

*Liu, Yü-hsia. "Study of the Bronze Casting Technique of the Yin Dynasty," *Preliminary Reports of Excavations at Anyang*, Part IV (Peking and Nanking, 1933), pp. 681–96.

Pelliot, Paul. "The Royal Tombs of Anyang," in *Independence, Convergence and Borrowing in Institution, Thought and Art*. Cambridge, Mass.: Harvard University Press, 1937.

*Pien, M. N. "On the Turtle Remains from the Archaeological Site of Anyang, Honan," *Bulletin of the Geological Society of China*, XVII, No. 1 (1937), 121–33.

Preliminary Reports of Excavations at Anyang. Peking and Nanking. Part I (1929), pp. 1–218; Part II (1930), pp. 219–422; Part III (1931), pp. 423–558; Part IV (1933), pp. 559–734.

Shan-hai-ching, ed. Kuo P'o. Ssu-pu-ts'ung-k'an edition. Shanghai: Commercial Press, 1919–29.

*Shih, Chang-ju. "On the Animal Remains from the Tombs of the Yin Dynasty at Hsiao-t'un, Anyang," *Bulletin of the College of Arts* (National Taiwan University), No. 5 (1954), pp. 1–14.

*Shih, Hsin-keng. *Preliminary Report on the Black Pottery Cultural Remains in the Second District in Hang Hsian*. Hangchow, 1938.

Teilhard de Chardin, P., and C. C. Young. "On the Mammalian Remains from the Archaeological Site of Anyang," *Palaeontologia Sinica*, Ser. C, Vol. VII, Fasc. 1 (1936).

*Tung, Tso-pin. "On the Seven Complete Inscribed Tortoise Shells from the Excavation at Hou-chia-chuang, Anyang," *T'ien-yeh-k'ao-ku-pao-kao*, No. 1 (1936), pp. 91–165.

*———. "On the Inscribed Plastron (No. 2908) Recording King Wu-ting's Hunting Expedition to 'Ch'iu' (𪊨)," *Continental Magazine*, Vol. VIII, No. 12.

Waley, Arthur. *The Life and Times of Po Chü-i*. London: George Allen & Unwin Ltd., 1949.

Weidenreich, Franz. "Dentition of Sinanthropus Pekinensis," *Palaeontologia Sinica*, New Ser. D, No. 1 (1937).

*In Chinese.

116

———. "On the Earliest Representatives of Modern Mankind Recovered on the Soil of East Asia," *Bulletin of the Natural History Society of Peking*, XIII (1939), 161–74.

———. *Apes, Giants and Man*. Chicago: University of Chicago Press, 1946.

Wu, G. D. *Prehistoric Pottery in China*. London: Kegan Paul, Trench, Trubner & Co., Ltd., 1938.

Yang-Teou-Wa. *Archaeologia Orientalis*, Ser. B, Vol. III (1942).

*Young, C. C., and T. S. Liu. "Further Notes on the Mammalian Remains of Yin-hsü, Anyang," *Chinese Journal of Archaeology*, IV (1949), 145–52.

*In Chinese.

Index

Index

Index